Georgia Cooking in an Oklahoma Kitchen

trisha yearwood

Georgia Cooking in an Oklahoma Kitchen

Recipes from My Family to Yours

with Gwen Yearwood
and Beth Yearwood Bernard
foreword by Garth Brooks

clarkson potter/publishers
new york

Copyright © 2008 by Trisha Yearwood
Photographs copyright © 2008 by Ben Fink

Originally published in hardcover in the United States by Clarkson Potter/
Publishers, an imprint of the Crown Publishing Group, a division of
Random House LLC, New York, in 2008

All photographs are by Ben Fink with the exception of those appearing on
pages 8 and 167 by Bev Parker and those appearing on pages 5, 47, 51, 75,
86, 96, 103, 106 (bottom), 117, 126, 153, 166, 175, 179, 193, and 205 from the
author's collection.

Library of Congress Cataloging-in-Publication Data
Yearwood, Trisha.
Georgia cooking in an Oklahoma kitchen : recipes from my
family to yours / Trisha Yearwood, with Gwen Yearwood
and Beth Bernard. — 1st ed.
p. cm.
Includes index.
1. Cookery, American—Southern style. 2. Cookery—Georgia.
I. Yearwood, Gwen. II. Bernard, Beth. III. Title.
TX715.2.S69Y43 2008
641.5975—dc22   2007024753

ISBN 978-0-8041-8662-9

Printed in the United States

BOOK DESIGN BY JENNIFER K. DAVIS BEAL
COVER DESIGN BY JENNIFER K. DAVIS BEAL
COVER PHOTOGRAPHY BY RUSS HARRINGTON

10 9 8 7 6 5 4 3 2 1

First Paperback Edition

dedication

In memory of
Jack Howard Yearwood,
a wonderful husband, father, friend,
and one hell of a good cook.
We miss you every second of every minute
of every day.

Love,
your girls,
Gwen, Beth, and Patricia

contents

OPPOSITE: Skillet Almond Shortbread (page 209)

foreword

Why is it that two people can make the same dish, following the same recipe from beginning to end, and one will taste ten times better than the other? We all judge food on how it smells and how it tastes, but when you find a dish that is amazing, there is always that "something" you can't describe. I believe that "something" is love. Loving to cook is the difference between making food that is good and food that is *great*.

Watching Miss Yearwood (as I often call my wife) in the kitchen, it is easy to see how much she loves to cook. In fact, she defines what loving to cook means to me. Peeling potatoes and snapping green beans are chores that I rush through to get them over with; Trisha looks upon these tasks not as chores but as the careful, loving steps she takes on the way to making a meal that will bring joy to whoever is seated at our table.

When I think of Thanksgiving or Christmas, it is always with the pleasure of knowing this year's meal will be amazing. The anticipation of the German chocolate cake she bakes each year for my birthday makes me not mind getting a year older. And I know how happy it makes her that all of our friends feel the same way, because she always makes their favorite cake, pie, or pudding for their special days, too.

Be it for family or guests, Trisha always wants the meal to be something worth remembering. Which brings me to this: To make truly delicious meals, not only must you love to cook, you must also love those for whom you are cooking. *That is what makes Miss Yearwood's cooking . . . simply the best*.

—Garth Brooks

introduction

Other than for the "singing thing" I do, I'm best known among my friends for my cooking. It's something I take great pride in. I don't think people expect me to be a good cook, so it's always fun to watch their expressions as they taste whatever I've made. Their liking my food gives me the same feeling I get when an audience applauds one of my performances—it feels good!

Food seems to always be a topic of conversation when my friends and I get together. Somebody's got some new recipe we all need to try, or we're talking about a new restaurant that's just opened and finding out if anyone's been there yet. Sharing recipes and memories about food has always been a great way to connect with friends and family.

When I first moved to Oklahoma, what I missed most of all was my family. We make every effort to see one another often, but there are those times when we can't get together, and I found myself on those lonely days making my mom's chicken noodle soup or baking a batch of my niece Ashley's banana bread. For my birthday a few years ago, my mom and my sister put together a notebook full of our favorite family recipes and called it *Georgia Recipes for an Oklahoma Kitchen*. Ashley even did artwork on her computer, using pictures of both states for the cover. We've come a long way from that binder full of typed recipes, and we found many "lost" or never-written-down recipes along the way.

That compilation planted the seed for this very special family cookbook. Some of these recipes go back to my grandmothers, Elizabeth Yearwood and Elizabeth "Lizzie" Paulk. I love the idea of making a meal I can imagine my grandmother Lizzie making for Grandaddy to enjoy when he came in from working the tobacco fields back in the 1930s. It's yet another way we stay connected from generation to generation. My mom, my sister, and I had a wonderful time organizing, compiling the recipes, and sometimes recreating an old recipe entirely to make it workable for modern kitchens and lives. You'll also find that the ones that do take a bit more time and effort, like the frosted birthday cakes and the super-huge Just Married Pound Cake, create wonderful memories you will share with your family for generations to come.

My sister and I have really high standards when it comes to cooking, because we learned from the best. Mama taught us the basics of cooking and to use what you have available. I think one of the biggest lessons she taught me is that it's okay to change a recipe to make it work for me. I used to follow every recipe to the letter, afraid that if I left out something or added something else, it wouldn't turn out right. She also taught us simple rules of thumb—the ratio of flour to fat to liquid in a white sauce or a biscuit dough, for example—that are at the heart of every successful recipe. I learned that as long as I observed those basic guidelines, I could change the rest around. My husband recently asked if we could try to create a heartier, meatier lasagna recipe, and I said, "Sure! Let's experiment." If it turns out well, maybe it'll make the next cookbook!

From my daddy I learned about laughing, having fun in the kitchen, and the satisfaction that comes from seeing the pleasure others take in a meal you have prepared. He was always happy when folks appreciated his cooking, and he passed that down to me. I think comfort food gets its name from the wonderful memories associated with specific meals. My daddy's barbecued chicken recipe still makes my mouth water when I think about all of those chicken-cues we had on the town square in Monticello when I was growing up. Other recipes, like the Chicken

CLOCKWISE (from top left): Kyle Bernard; Bret Bernard and Beth; Joanne Jordan; Gwen, brother Wilson Paulk; John Bernard, Beth, Trisha, Gwen, and Joanne; Betty Maxwell; Ashley Bernard and Gwen; Trisha
CENTER: Beth, Trisha, Gwen, and Joanne

Broccoli Casserole, always bring a smile to my face because I know how much my family loves it when they find out that's what's for supper.

You'll also love how easy everything in this book is to make. I never want to try something new if I think it's going to take all day to cook. Who has time for that? These are easy-to-make recipes that use everyday seasonings you already have in your kitchen. Don't worry that I'll send you to a gourmet store to buy one specialty spice you'll never use again. As far as I'm concerned, there's really not much you can't do with a little salt and pepper—and maybe a jalapeño thrown in occasionally!

Garth says my cooking is good because it's made with love. I used to think that was just a sweet thing to say to your wife, but now I think it's true. If you truly love what you do, it shows—in life, love, good music, and good food. I hope you will love using these recipes as much as my family and I have enjoyed sharing them with the people who are important to us.

Trisha

Useful Equipment

In many of my recipes I've included suggestions about pan sizes, ingredient substitutions, information sources, and so on. This is a list of my favorite small appliances and kitchen gadgets and why they're my choices.

1. **Measuring spoons.** Three sets of metal spoons that include a $1/2$ tablespoon measurement. Choose sets that can be separated and stored each one with its equal. No need to wash an entire set when you've used only one.

2. **Measuring cups.** Two sets of dry measuring cups and 2 sets for liquid measuring. To dry-measure, overfill the cup and then scrape off the excess evenly with a flat-edged knife or spatula. Liquid measure has space above the top line and is easily read at eye level. OXO has designed liquid measuring cups that allow you to view the liquid from the top. No bending over!

3. **Cookie sheets.** Two cookie sheets of your choosing that fit in your oven with 2 inches of space on all sides. Sheets with a dark, nonstick finish bake a browner, crispier cookie, especially on the bottom, more quickly than a light, shiny sheet. An insulated sheet bakes a softer cookie. Don't wash insulated sheets in the dishwasher or soak in dishwater.

4. **Jelly roll pan.** Two pans with low sides, $1/2$ to 1 inch deep. Even if you never bake a jelly roll, these pans are a must for recipes that have juicy drippings, such as Roasted Carrots (page 123). They can also be used for baking cookies or biscuits.

5. **Fat separator or basting bulb.** The ideal way to remove fat from broth is to allow the broth to cool and then chill it so the fat solidifies and can be lifted off. If you don't have the time, fat can be removed from hot broth by lowering a ladle just below the fat line and allowing the fat to flow into the ladle. A fat separator is a clear, heat-resistant cup with a spout coming out from the side near the bottom. When the cup is tilted, the broth pours off, leaving the fat behind. You can get the same effect with a basting bulb. Squeeze the bulb to expel the air before plunging the tube to the bottom of the broth. Release the bulb, and the broth is drawn up into the tube, leaving the fat.

6. **Electric stand mixer.** KitchenAid with attachments that include a flat beater, wire whip, food grinder, and roto slicer with shredder. Two mixer bowls are handy when things such as egg whites are to be beaten separately.

7. **Kitchen blender.** Choose a brand such as Oster that has a glass, square-topped pitcher for even blending and ease of cleaning.

8. **Electric skillet.** Rival 12 x 15 x 3-inch pan with a cover. Temperature control is useful for frying chicken or cooking pancakes.

9. **Slow cookers.** One large, 4-quart, for cooking and keeping bigger batches of food warm, and a smaller, such as Rival 1-pint dip pot for hot dips. A removable liner makes cleanup easy.

10. **Pressure cooker.** Four to 6-quart. Mine is 6-quart because I make lots of creamed potatoes.

11. **Roasting pan with rack and cover.** Should be large enough to hold a 20-pound turkey or ham. Cameron manufactures a heavy-duty stainless-steel pan with a flat top that can be used as a separate pan. The handles of the pan and top are offset, making this very large cooker easier to store.

12. **Digital kitchen scale.** Salter weighs amounts up to 11 pounds.

13. **Cookie press.** Manual Mirro press with attachments.

14. **Cast-iron Dutch oven.**

15. **Cast-iron skillet.** Nine or 10 inches in diameter. Directions for seasoning are usually included with the pan. They are also given in this cookbook following the Buttermilk Cornbread recipe (p. 154).

16. **Electric ice-cream churn.** Wooden bucket with a tall metal canister that holds 1 gallon.

Substitutions and Helpful Hints

- 1 tablespoon = 3 teaspoons
- 1 tablespoon flour = $1\frac{1}{2}$ teaspoons cornstarch
- 1 cup self-rising flour = 1 cup sifted all-purpose flour + $1\frac{1}{2}$ teaspoons baking powder + $\frac{1}{8}$ teaspoon salt
- 1 cup buttermilk = 1 tablespoon lemon juice or white vinegar + enough milk to make 1 cup
- Half-and-half = $1\frac{1}{2}$ tablespoons melted butter + enough whole milk to make 1 cup
- 1 teaspoon vinegar = 2 teaspoons lemon juice
- Make 1 cup confectioners' sugar by streaming $\frac{3}{4}$ cup granulated sugar into the small opening of a blender set at high speed.
- To correct an oversalted soup or stew, add a couple of peeled and quartered white potatoes and cook.
- When selecting cuts of meat, such as hams and roasts, allow 8 ounces, uncooked, per person.

snacks and appetizers

Everybody in my family LOVES good food. We're not much into finger foods because they're just too dainty for us—those tiny servings are usually just enough to whet our appetites! These dips and snacks are so hearty they should probably be called fist foods. I remember how, back when Mama made wedding cakes for extra income, she would also sometimes make cocktail foods for the wedding reception. My sister and I would usually go along to help carry the cake. Beth, being the oldest, was in charge of sitting in the backseat of the station wagon and holding the top layer of the wedding cake, the one with the bride and groom on top. She never dropped one! My job was usually holding one of the bottom layers that could be repaired easily at the church if it got dented along the way. At the reception, I would watch in amazement as people took one or two cheese straws and maybe one sausage hors d'oeuvre, and think that if I could make my own plate, I would pile it high with those yummy treats. Maybe that's where it all began for me, knowing that if I could learn to make this wonderful food myself, I could eat as much of it as I wanted. I have been known, for instance, to make an entire batch of sausage hors d'oeuvres when nobody at all was coming over!

Any of the recipes in this chapter are great whether you have a big party planned, a small gathering of family trickling in for the holidays, or if you're just craving something good!

Cheese Straws

Makes 4 dozen

From Gwen:
If you find a Mirro cookie press, either vintage or new, that includes the star tube, grab it!

I *love* cheese! I would eat a piece of Cheddar cheese over a piece of chocolate cake any day. That probably makes me a little weird, but if you love cheese like I do, you'll love these cheese straws. My mom used to make them for baby showers and wedding receptions. In 1991, the year my career started to really take off, she made them for me to give as Christmas gifts to everyone who had been so supportive. We laughed about how these cheesy treats were baked in a small kitchen in Monticello, Georgia, and ended up on the desks of some of the biggest movers and shakers in Nashville.

3   10-ounce bricks sharp Cheddar cheese, room temperature

1   cup (2 sticks) butter, softened

4   cups sifted all-purpose flour

2   teaspoons salt

⅛   teaspoon black pepper

⅛   teaspoon cayenne pepper

Dash of garlic powder

Preheat the oven to 325°F.

Put the softened cheese and butter in the bowl of a heavy-duty electric mixer. Using the heaviest mixer attachment, beat the cheese and butter until the mixture has the consistency of whipped cream, about 30 minutes.

On a sheet of waxed paper, sift 3 cups of the flour with the salt, black pepper, cayenne, and garlic powder. Gradually add the seasoned flour to the cheese mixture by large spoonfuls, beating well after each addition. Add the unseasoned flour until the dough is somewhat stiff but still soft enough to be pushed through a cookie press; you may not need to add all of the flour.

Lightly spray a cookie sheet with cooking spray. Put a portion of the dough into a cookie press fitted with the star tube and press the dough onto the cookie sheet in long strips that run the length of the pan (see Note). Bake for 20 minutes. The cheese straws should be golden brown and crisp. With a sharp knife, cut the long strips into 3-inch lengths. Use a flat, thin spatula or egg turner to remove the cheese straws from the pan. Allow them to cool on a wire rack. When they are completely cool, store in a tightly covered container.

Note: If you don't have a cookie press, form the dough into 1-inch balls and flatten them with a fork.

Sausage Hors d'Oeuvres

Makes 50

I've laughed a lot while writing this cookbook—and gotten very hungry! I laugh because most people consider these tasty meat-balls the perfect small bite for a party or wedding reception, but I sometimes make them just to satisfy a craving! They are usually served cold, but when I make them at home, I serve them warm, right out of the oven, and they are awesome! So to answer the burning question, can you make an entire meal out of sausage ball appetizers? *Yes!*

From Beth:
Double this recipe, bake, and freeze half for use at a later time.

1 pound spicy pork sausage

10 ounces Cheddar cheese, grated

3 cups baking mix, such as Bisquick, or self-rising flour

Salt and pepper

From Trisha:
I like Jimmy Dean's sage sausage for this recipe.

Preheat the oven to 375°F.

Using a stand mixer fitted with the paddle attachment, combine the sausage, cheese, and baking mix and beat on low speed until blended. Add salt and pepper to taste. Shape the mixture into 1-inch balls and place them 1 inch apart on an ungreased cookie sheet. Bake for 20 minutes, or until browned. Drain on paper towels, and serve hot, warm, or at room temperature.

Kim's Black-Eyed Pea Dip

I'm sort of a snob when it comes to trying new recipes. I just seem to like my old tried and true ones best, and it takes a lot for something new to grab my attention. I had to have the recipe for this dip after I tried it on Super Bowl Sunday 2006. Garth is a die-hard Steelers fan, so it was an exciting day. Everybody always brings something for the party, and this was my friend Kim's contribution. Being a good southern girl, I love anything with black-eyed peas in it, but for you folks who are right now turning up your noses at the idea of eating black-eyed peas, all I can say is just try it. In fact, maybe I should name it something else for those skeptics. How about Pea Dippy?

 3 15-ounce cans black-eyed peas, rinsed and drained

½ cup finely chopped canned pickled jalapeños, juices reserved

10 ounces Cheddar cheese, grated

 1 medium sweet onion, finely chopped

¼ cup (½ stick) butter, softened

¼ teaspoon garlic powder

In an electric mixer or large mixing bowl, mix together the peas, jalapeños, 3 tablespoons of the reserved jalapeño juice, Cheddar, onion, butter, and garlic powder until blended. Heat the dip in a medium Crock-Pot and serve it warm with corn chips.

Warm Feta Dip with Artichokes

Spinach artichoke dips seem to be on every restaurant's appetizer list these days, and I like them okay but have never been a big spinach fan. Feta cheese, on the other hand, is something I'm very fond of, so I was excited to find this recipe. It's also one of those really easy recipes that tastes like it must have been really hard to make. You gotta love those!

Serves 8

1 14-ounce can artichoke hearts, drained and finely chopped

5 ounces feta cheese, crumbled

¾ cup mayonnaise

½ cup grated Parmesan cheese

1 2-ounce jar pimientos, drained and diced

2 teaspoons minced garlic

   Pita chips or Melba toast, for dipping

Preheat the oven to 350°F.

In a medium bowl, stir together the artichoke hearts, feta cheese, mayonnaise, Parmesan cheese, pimientos, and garlic until thoroughly combined. Transfer the mixture to a small casserole or glass pie plate and bake, uncovered, for 25 minutes, or until lightly browned. To serve, place the dish on a larger platter and surround with pita chips or Melba toast.

Ranch Dressing Cheese Ball

Makes 2 cheese balls; serves 24

From Beth:
Let this sit at room temperature for about 30 minutes before serving for easier spreading.

This is my sister's go-to appetizer for church socials, Super Bowl Sundays, and Christmas munchies. Several years ago, she put too much of the ranch dressing mix into the recipe, and it was hard to serve. My dad renamed it the "cheese wad." We think Ranch Dressing Cheese Ball sounds more appetizing, but at our house, it will forever be known as Cheese Wad!

1   4-ounce package Hidden Valley Ranch dressing mix

½   cup mayonnaise

½   cup buttermilk, well shaken

16   ounces Cheddar cheese, grated, room temperature

12   ounces cream cheese, room temperature

1   cup pecans, finely chopped

In a medium bowl, combine the dressing mix, mayonnaise, buttermilk, Cheddar, and cream cheese until thoroughly blended. Divide the mixture into two equal portions in two separate bowls. Cover the bowls and place them in the freezer for 30 minutes. When each portion is firm, use your hands to shape it into a ball. Place the nuts in a shallow bowl or on a piece of waxed paper. Roll each ball in the nuts to coat it on all sides. Serve with crackers or bagel chips.

Pimiento Cheese Spread

A pimiento cheese sandwich made on very fresh white bread is a true southern staple. Nothing goes better with Gwen's Fried Chicken (page 93). Mama slices the crusts off the sandwiches and cuts them in half for family reunions—very southern belle!

Makes 4 cups

From Gwen: Make a lot of these. One triangle disappears in only three bites!

2 7-ounce jars canned, sliced pimientos, drained

3 10-ounce bricks sharp Cheddar cheese, finely grated

1 cup mayonnaise

Place the drained pimientos in a blender or food processor and purée until smooth. Using an electric mixer, combine the cheese and pimiento, beating until smooth. Beat in the mayonnaise. Spread on slices of white sandwich bread while the mixture is room temperature. Trim the bread crusts and cut the sandwiches into triangles.

The spread may be stored, covered, in the refrigerator for up to 1 week. Remove the spread from the refrigerator and allow it to reach room temperature before serving.

His 'n' Hers Deviled Eggs

Makes 24

You won't go to a southern picnic or covered-dish supper and *not* see deviled eggs. Garth and I grew up eating different versions of this dish, so both varieties are included here. Honestly, I never met a deviled egg I didn't like, so these are both yummy to me!

12 large eggs

His Filling
¼ cup mayonnaise

2 teaspoons yellow mustard

1 tablespoon butter, softened

Salt and pepper to taste

Her Filling
¼ cup mayonnaise

1½ tablespoons sweet pickle relish

1 teaspoon yellow mustard

Salt and pepper to taste

Paprika for garnish

From Trisha: Cool, crack, and peel the eggs like the recipe says, or your yolks will turn green on the outside! I guess that's where green eggs and ham came from.

Place the eggs in a medium saucepan with water to cover and bring to a boil. Remove from the heat, cover the pan, and let stand for 20 minutes. Pour off the hot water and refill the saucepan with cold water. Crack the eggsshells all over and let them sit in the cold water for 5 minutes. Peel the eggs, cover, and chill for at least 1 hour.

Halve the eggs lengthwise. Carefully remove the yolks and transfer them to a small bowl. Mash the yolks with a fork, then stir in the filling ingredients of your choice. Season with salt and pepper. Scoop a spoonful of the mixture into each egg white half. Sprinkle the tops with paprika.

This is one time when freshest isn't bestest. Very fresh eggs are hard to peel, so use eggs near the sell-by date on the carton. Also, invert each egg in the carton the night before cooking so the yolk will become more centered in the white. It makes a prettier deviled egg. Who knew?

Boiled Peanuts

If you've ever driven through a small town in Georgia, you no doubt have seen signs for boiled peanuts along the roadside. I've found that they're a love-hate thing; people are rarely undecided about boiled peanuts! I include the recipe here because I absolutely love them. When I make them at home in Oklahoma, it takes me back to our family vacation trips to Florida, when we'd stop on the roadside and eat the warm peanuts in the car. Yum!

Makes 10 cups

5   pounds fresh green peanuts

Salt

Wash the peanuts and put them in a 3-quart stockpot. Add enough water to barely float the peanuts, measuring the amount of water required. Add ⅔ cup salt for each gallon of water used. Stir to distribute the salt. Bring the water to a boil and reduce the heat to medium. Cover the pan and cook the peanuts for 1½ hours, or until the shelled peanuts are tender. Add water during cooking if the peanuts are no longer floating in the liquid. Remove from the heat and cool in the cooking liquid.

From Gwen:
Use green peanuts for this. Dried nuts in the shell are just not as tender.

The peanuts will become saltier as they sit in the liquid, so taste them at intervals as they are cooling. When they are as salty as you like them, drain the peanuts (do not rinse) and store them in the refrigerator or freezer. (If the boiled peanuts are too salty, soak them in plain water to dilute the saltiness.)

Green Punch

Makes 20 cups

Serve this punch with Cheese Straws (page 20). It's a Yearwood family tradition—perfect to serve at Christmas parties, because it's a beautiful bright green and makes a pretty punch bowl.

- 2 .13-ounce packets unsweetened lemon-lime soft drink mix, such as Kool-Aid
- 2 cups sugar
- 1 46-ounce can pineapple juice
- 12 ounces frozen lemonade concentrate, thawed
- 32 ounces (1 quart) ginger ale

Put 2 quarts of water in a 1-gallon container. Add the drink mix and sugar and stir until the sugar is dissolved. Add the pineapple juice and lemonade concentrate and stir well. Just before serving, add the ginger ale.

From Gwen: Monticello ladies often act as hostesses for everything from bridal showers to baby showers. This easy punch is a favorite for those occasions.

Jerry's Sugared Pecans

I think making someone else's recipes is a wonderful way to remember them when they're no longer with us. Garth's brother Jerry loved my cooking, and he was a good cook himself. He always made me feel he truly appreciated the meals I made for him, and I loved him for it. He had a wonderful smile and a great spirit. Jerry brought these pecans out to the house one day, and I only stopped eating them when they were gone! The butter and sugar make them crunchy, sweet, and rich.

½ cup (1 stick) butter, melted

3 large egg whites

1 cup sugar

1 teaspoon ground cinnamon

4 cups pecan halves

Preheat the oven to 350°F.

Line a large baking sheet with sides with aluminum foil. Pour the butter onto the lined sheet. In a large bowl, mix the egg whites, sugar, and cinnamon. Add the pecan halves and toss until they are fully coated. Spread the pecans onto the baking sheet. Bake for 30 minutes, stirring the pecans every 10 minutes. Cool on the baking sheet for 10 to 15 minutes before serving.

Makes 4 cups

From Gwen: These pecans will still be a bit wet and gooey when you take them out of the oven. As they cool on the baking sheet, they will get crunchy.

Grandma Yearwood's Sweet Iceberg Pickles

Makes 6 quarts

From Gwen: Chill before serving. Store leftover pickles in the refrigerator.

Note: Five tablespoons mixed pickling spices may be used instead of the individual spices.

These are sweet and crunchy, like no other pickle I've ever tasted. They're great on salads, but I eat them right out of the jar with a fork!

3 cups pickling lime (see Note on page 36)

7 pounds small cucumbers (no bigger than 1 inch in diameter), unpeeled, sliced crosswise ⅛ inch thick

5 pounds sugar

6 cups apple cider vinegar

1 tablespoon whole cloves

1 ounce fresh ginger

1 tablespoon whole allspice berries

1 tablespoon celery seed

2 cinnamon sticks, broken into pieces

Mix 2 gallons water with the lime in a 3-gallon stockpot. Add the cucumbers, stir, and soak for 24 hours, stirring occasionally to redistribute the lime.

Stir the pickles and drain the lime water. Replace the lime water with 2 gallons fresh water. Some lime will remain in the pickles at this point. Soak for 1 hour, then drain and replace with fresh water again. Continue soaking the pickles in fresh water and draining every hour until the pickles have soaked in fresh water for 4 hours. Drain again.

In a separate large saucepan, mix the sugar and vinegar. Place the cloves, ginger, allspice, celery seed, and cinnamon on a square of cheesecloth and bring the sides in to make a small bag; tie it closed with cotton string or thread (see Note at left). Bring the vinegar mixture to a boil and pour it (including the cheesecloth bundle) over the

continued . . .

pickles. Bring the pickles and vinegar to a boil. Remove from the heat and let stand overnight.

The next day, bring the pickles back to a boil and simmer for 1 hour. Wash and rinse 12 1-pint canning jars. Fill the jars with pickles and liquid, leaving ½ inch head space at the top of each jar. Wipe the edges of the jars and close with canning lids and rings, hand-tightening each. Seal the jars in a hot-water bath (instructions follow) or in a large pressure canner, following the manufacturer's instructions.

Note: You can find pickling lime in the canning section of a grocery store, or ask at your local farmer's market. You can also order pickling lime at www.kitchen krafts.com and www.canning pantry.com.

Hot-Water Bath Method for Sealing Canning Jars

Place a wire rack with handles in the bottom of a large, deep pot with a lid. The rack will keep the jars off the bottom of the pot, and the handles make it easier to add and remove the jars. Fill the pot half full of water and bring to a boil. Lower the jars slowly and carefully into the water. The water should cover the jars by 1 inch. Add more boiling water if necessary to reach this level. Cover the pot and boil the jars for 30 minutes after the water has returned to a boil. Carefully remove the jars from the water and set aside to cool. The jar lids will pop and invert as they seal.

When the jars are cool, remove the rings if the pickles are to be stored before use. The rings may rust during lengthy storage, making them difficult to remove. When the rings are removed, the jars should be wiped clean and handled in such a way as not to disturb the sealed lid. Lift by the sides or the glass rim only.

Vi's Garlic Dill Pickles

If you're not a sweet pickle fan, you should try these wonderful dill pickles that my friend Lisa's grandmother makes. Sweet pickles are generally sliced, but these are served whole. They are deliciously dilled and better than any store-bought pickle, I guarantee it!

Makes 5 to 6 quarts

12   large sprigs fresh dill

 6   garlic cloves, peeled

 6   pounds small cucumbers, no more than 1 inch in diameter

 2   cups cider vinegar

½   cup sugar

½   cup rock salt

Wash and rinse 6 1-quart canning jars. Place a sprig of dill and a clove of garlic in the bottom of each jar. Pack the cucumbers into the jars and place a large sprig of dill on top of each. In a saucepan, combine 1½ quarts water and the vinegar, sugar, and salt. Bring to a boil, then remove from the heat. Pour the vinegar mixture over the cucumbers. Wipe the tops of the jars and close with canning lids and rings. Seal the jars by processing in a hot-water bath (page 36) for 3 minutes.

From Gwen:
I first ate these wonderful pickles when Lisa brought them to supper in Oklahoma. Those large sprigs of dill were beautiful in the jar.

soups and salads

There's nothing like walking into the kitchen on a cold, rainy day and smelling a warm, inviting soup simmering on the stove. I love soup, all kinds of soup. I love soups with thin broth and rich, hearty soups that are meals all by themselves. Because a soup is only as good as the broth it is based on, we give our recipe for homemade boiled hen and broth, which we use to make chicken and dumplings, among many other soothing, homey soups.

Any of these salads would make a nice meal with a warm bowl of soup. Because I like a lot of texture and interest in my salads, you'll find many of these have something extra thrown in at the end, like a sprinkle of bacon or chopped nuts or sunflower seeds. The southern nut of choice is most often the pecan (here and throughout the book), but I would encourage you to try almonds, walnuts, or whatever nut strikes your fancy. Served on their own or paired up, these soups and salads will leave you satisfied!

Lizzie's Chicken and Dumplings

From Gwen: My mom would drape the dough strips over her fingers as she transferred the pieces to the broth. It was fun for me, many years later, to allow my grandchildren to handle the dough the same way.

My grandmother, Lizzie Paulk, was an amazing woman. She worked the fields in South Georgia with my grandfather Winnes, raised three children, and somehow still found time to put three home-cooked meals on the table every single day. She passed away when I was in junior high, but I have wonderful memories of her laughter and her love for her family. Mama had always complained she could never get her dumplings to come out as thin as her mom's, but the first time she made them after Grandma died, she said it was as if Lizzie were guiding her. Maybe she finally decided it was okay for Mama to be able to make her dumplings! They've come out perfectly every time since. (See photo, page 10.)

1　5-pound hen (makes about 4 pounds cooked, after bones and skin are removed)

1　tablespoon salt

1　teaspoon pepper

Dumplings

2　cups unsifted all-purpose flour

1　teaspoon salt

¾　cup water

　　Salt and pepper

Put the hen, breast side down, in a very large (8-quart) stockpot and add water to within 2 inches of the top of the pot; this will vary according to the size of your pot, but the hen should float clear of the bottom of the pot and be covered completely. Add the salt and pepper. Bring the water to a boil and reduce the heat to simmer. Cover the pot and cook for 2 hours, or until the chicken is tender and the drumstick joint twists easily. Allow the chicken and broth to cool slightly, and then remove the chicken to a colander.

Strain the broth into a very large bowl. Cover the broth and place it in the refrigerator. When the fat solidifies on the top of the broth, remove and discard it. Remove the chicken from the bones and cut or shred the meat by hand into small pieces. Set aside 2 cups and refrigerate or freeze the rest for another use. (Leftover broth may also be frozen in individual containers to be used another time.)

To make the dumplings, heat 2 quarts of the defatted chicken broth in a 3-quart saucepan. While it heats, put the flour in a medium bowl. Dissolve the salt in the water and stir the mixture into the flour to make a stiff dough. Turn the dough out onto a heavily floured surface and knead until smooth, 1 to 2 minutes. Divide it into 4 parts. Heavily flour a rolling pin. Roll one portion of the dough very thin. With a very sharp knife or pizza cutter, cut the dough into 2 x 4-inch strips.

When the broth reaches a rolling boil, add the strips of dough. Reduce the heat to a simmer, cover the pot, and roll out another portion of dough, cut it into strips, and drop them into the broth. Continue preparing each portion of the dough and adding the strips in this manner. Always raise the heat to bring the broth back to a rolling boil before dropping in more dough strips, and then reduce the heat to simmer before covering the pot again. Sprinkle in the salt and pepper to taste. Add the 2 cups of cooked chicken and cover the pan. Simmer for 15 minutes.

Many cookbooks assume we all know the basics of cooking, and instructions for boiling a hen, like you'll find in this recipe, are seldom included. When I first moved away from home and started asking my mom for recipes, I needed her help with everything from boiling corn on the cob to making chicken broth from scratch. If I don't use all the broth from a hen in the recipe I'm making, or if I'm just cooking the chicken to use in a salad, I save the broth and freeze it for the future. Canned chicken broth is good, but homemade is always better! A hen is a mature chicken that produces eggs. A fryer is a younger, more tender chicken. Using a hen for chicken stock gives you a richer broth, because hens have more fat than fryers. Mama taught me that!

Mama's Awesome Chicken Noodle Soup

Serves 10

From Gwen:
I would never have guessed that sending this simple soup would bring such pleasure to my child and to me!

I love living in Oklahoma. I do miss my family in Georgia, but luckily I get to travel back and forth a lot for visits. My Georgia family has also made the trek to Oklahoma several times, so now both places feel like home. Only once have I gotten so homesick I thought I wouldn't make it, and that was because I was really sick with the flu and Mama wasn't there to take care of me. Sometimes nobody will do except Mama! She made this soup for me, froze it in quart containers, packed it in dry ice (who knew you could get dry ice in Monticello?), and shipped it overnight to me in a Styrofoam cooler. When I got it the next morning, I cried, ate some soup, cried, ate some more soup, and thanked God for the most awesome mom on the planet!

1   4-pound hen

3   celery stalks with leafy tops, chopped

3   carrots, peeled and chopped

3   garlic cloves, sliced

1   large sweet onion, such as Vidalia, chopped

2   tablespoons salt

½   teaspoon black pepper

½   teaspoon chopped fresh parsley

2   bay leaves

1   16-ounce package frozen green peas

8   ounces noodles, such as egg noodles or very thin spaghetti, broken into small pieces

Put the hen in a large stockpot and pour in water to cover (about 8 cups). Add the celery, carrots, garlic, onion, salt, pepper, parsley, and bay leaves. Bring to a boil over high heat, then immediately reduce the heat to a simmer. Skim off any foam that rises to the surface. Simmer the hen for 2 hours, or until the meat comes off the bone easily. Remove the hen to a large bowl and cool. Strain the broth into a large bowl and discard the vegetables. Chill the broth and skim off and discard any fat that has risen to the top.

When the chicken is cool enough to handle, remove the meat from the bones, discarding the bones and skin, and shred the meat into bite-sized pieces.

Return the broth to a large pot. Add the shredded chicken, the frozen peas, and the noodles. Bring the soup to a boil, then simmer over medium heat for 10 minutes, or until the pasta is tender. Add extra salt to taste if desired.

Trisha's Chicken Tortilla Soup

Serves 8

Chicken tortilla soup became really popular in restaurants a few years ago, but it was never something I made at home. Garth loves this soup and orders it almost every time he sees it on a menu, so I started studying the different versions at each restaurant and questioning Garth about what he liked and didn't like about each one. This recipe I finally came up with doesn't actually taste like any of those we tasted in restaurants, but we love it—and now we can enjoy it whenever we want!

3   tablespoons butter

1   teaspoon minced garlic

1   medium onion, finely chopped

2   tablespoons all-purpose flour

3   14-ounce cans chicken broth

4   cups half-and-half

1   10.75-ounce can cream of chicken soup

1   cup prepared salsa, mild or spicy, according to your taste

4   boneless, skinless chicken breasts, boiled, drained, and shredded

1   15-ounce can kidney beans, drained

1   15-ounce can black beans, drained

1   15-ounce can whole kernel corn, drained

2   teaspoons ground cumin

1   1.27-ounce packet fajita seasoning

1   16-ounce bag tortilla chips

8   ounces Monterey Jack cheese, grated

8   ounces sharp Cheddar cheese, grated

½   cup sour cream

Melt the butter in a large pot over medium heat; add the garlic and onion and sauté for 5 minutes, or until softened. Add the flour and stir well, cooking for 1 minute more. Add the broth and the half-and-half. Bring to a boil over medium heat, about 10 minutes, then reduce the heat to low. Stir in the cream of chicken soup, salsa, chicken, beans, corn, cumin, and fajita seasoning. Continue to simmer over low heat for 15 minutes. Crumble the tortilla chips into individual bowls and top with a ladle of soup. Sprinkle each serving with cheese and add a dollop of sour cream.

Jack's Brunswick Stew

My daddy was a great cook, and many of the recipes in this cookbook are his. If there was a fund-raiser in Monticello, people would always ask, "Is Jack making the Brunswick Stew?" or "Is Jack cooking the chickens?" before they bought their tickets. The food was usually prepared outside in very large quantities with the help of members of the sponsoring organization. Brunswick Stew is one of those classic southern dishes that varies from region to region, but I've never had Brunswick Stew that tasted like my dad's. In his version, everything is ground through a food grinder, so it's more like a wonderfully rich soup than a stew. His version also fed 160 people, so we've reduced our recipe to serve a cozy 16!

1	pound Boston butt pork roast
1	pound fresh chicken or hen, bone in
1	pound boneless beef chuck roast
1	pound red or white potatoes
1	small (3 ounces) sweet onion, such as Vidalia
6	cups canned tomatoes
2½	teaspoons salt
2½	teaspoons ground black pepper
⅛	teaspoon ground cayenne (red) pepper
¾	cup ketchup
2	tablespoons Worcestershire sauce
32	ounces (4 cups) cream-style white corn

Place the pork and chicken in a 1½-gallon stockpot with water to cover. Bring to a boil, then immediately reduce the heat to a simmer. Skim off any foam that rises to the top and cook for 2 hours, or until the meat is very tender, skimming occasionally. Remove the meat to a bowl and reserve the stock.

At the same time, place the beef in a separate large stockpot with water to cover and cook for 2 hours, or until tender. Remove the beef and discard the broth.

Peel, quarter, and cook the potatoes in water until tender (see Note).

Remove and discard the bones and skin from all the cooked meat, and grind the meat with a heavy-duty meat grinder. Put 2 pints of the pork and chicken stock into a 1½-gallon stockpot. (Reserve the rest for another use.) Add the ground meats to the stock.

Peel and grind the onion and add it to the meat mixture. Grind the tomatoes, add them to the stockpot, and bring the mixture to a boil. When the stew is hot, grind and blend in the cooked potatoes, stirring until any lumps are removed. At this point, the stew should be soupy but not watery. If the stew is too thick to stir easily with a flat spatula or pancake turner, thin it slightly with the reserved pork and chicken stock.

Stir in the salt. Dissolve the black pepper and cayenne pepper in 1 tablespoon water, then add to the stew along with the ketchup and Worcestershire sauce. Cook for 30 minutes, stirring constantly.

Grind and add the corn, then continue to cook the stew over very low heat for 1 hour, stirring often and scraping the bottom of the stockpot with a flat spatula or pancake turner to avoid scorching.

Note: Cooking the potatoes before grinding them makes the stew cook more quickly. This method also makes the stew smoother and gives it the signature texture only Jack's stew has.

Daddy stirring Brunswick Stew for 160 people!

Winter Vegetable Soup

Serves 6

From Gwen:
If you're lucky enough to have a ham hock, cook it in water for seasoning instead of chicken broth.

Some recipes in this book have been passed down from generation to generation, and some are newer recipes discovered in the past few years that have become family classics. This is one of the old-timers. My mom used to make this soup when I was a child, and I remember how much my dad loved it served over biscuits. For me, when a recipe has a great memory attached to it, it tastes even better. I make this soup at the first sign of cold weather every year and serve it poured over Buttermilk Cornbread.

2   14-ounce cans chicken broth

3   red potatoes, about 4 ounces each, peeled and diced into ¾-inch pieces

1   12-ounce can diced tomatoes

1   8-ounce package frozen lima beans

2   tablespoons finely chopped onion

1   12-ounce can cream-style corn

   Salt and pepper to taste

In a medium saucepan, combine the broth with the potatoes, tomatoes, beans, and onion. Bring to a boil, then reduce the heat and cook the soup over medium heat for 20 to 25 minutes, or until the potatoes are tender. Remove from the heat, stir in the corn, and serve. Salt and pepper to taste. This soup goes great with Buttermilk Cornbread (page 154).

Baked Potato Soup

Serves 10

From Beth:
For a pretty presentation, top individual bowls of soup with a sprinkling of shredded cheese, crumbled bacon, and chopped green onions.

The best description I can offer of my sister's baked potato soup is that it tastes just like the best potato bar you ever tried. I always used to love twice-baked potatoes, mainly because the work of "fixing" a baked potato with the sour cream, cheese, and so on, was all done for you. It's the same with this soup. It's like someone fixed the ultimate baked potato just for you and put it into a bowl. All you have to do is enjoy it.

4   large baking potatoes

6   bacon slices

$\frac{2}{3}$ cup ($1\frac{1}{3}$ sticks) butter

$\frac{2}{3}$ cup all-purpose flour

6   cups milk

$\frac{3}{4}$ teaspoon salt

$\frac{1}{2}$ teaspoon pepper

2   green onions (scallions), finely chopped

5   ounces Cheddar cheese, shredded

8   ounces sour cream

Preheat the oven to 400°F.

Wash the potatoes and prick them several times with a fork. Wrap them individually in foil, and bake them for 1 hour, or until they are soft when squeezed (see Note). Let the potatoes cool slightly.

While the potatoes bake, cook the bacon in a small skillet, in a microwave, or on an indoor grill until crisp. Drain the bacon on paper towels and, when cool enough to handle, crumble it into small pieces. Set aside.

In a large, heavy saucepan, melt the butter over low heat. Add the flour, stirring constantly for 1 minute until smooth. Gradually whisk in the milk and cook over medium heat, stirring constantly, for 5 to 10 minutes, until the mixture is thick and bubbling. Cut the potatoes in half lengthwise, and scoop the flesh into the thickened milk mixture. Add the salt, pepper, green onions, reserved bacon, and Cheddar. Cook over low heat just until heated through. Stir in the sour cream and serve.

Note: Wrapping the potatoes in foil before baking makes them cook faster. To shorten the preparation time even more, peel the potatoes, cut them into 1-inch cubes, and cook them in a pressure cooker for 5 minutes. Leftover baked potatoes may also be used for this recipe. Peel and mash them coarsely before adding to the milk mixture.

Bret, Ashley, and Kyle Bernard

Potato Salad

When it comes to potato salad, you like what you like. This recipe is mayonnaise-based, but if you like a mustard-based potato salad, just experiment a little. Add some yellow mustard and leave out a little bit of the mayonnaise. Make these recipes your own by finding out what works for you. Our traditional potato salad uses peeled potatoes, but unpeeled work too, and the skins add some color to your dish.

5   pounds red potatoes, peeled and cut in ½-inch cubes

2   teaspoons salt, plus more to taste

4   hard-boiled eggs, peeled, and diced

¾   cup mayonnaise

½   cup sweet pickle relish

   Black pepper

Serves 12

From Gwen: Don't overcook the potatoes. They should hold their shape during mixing.

Place the potatoes in a medium saucepan or pressure cooker (see Note). Add 2 teaspoons salt and enough water to cover the potatoes. Boil the potatoes for 30 minutes, or until they are tender when pierced with the point of a knife but hold their shape. Drain the potatoes, transfer them to a large mixing bowl, and allow them to cool completely. Add the chopped eggs, mayonnaise, and sweet relish, and fold gently to combine. Add salt and pepper to taste. Refrigerate until ready to serve.

Note: The potatoes may be cooked in a pressure cooker. Sprinkle salt over the potatoes. Follow the manufacturer's instructions and pressure-cook for 5 minutes. Release the pressure immediately and drain and cool the potatoes.

Fourth of July Coleslaw

Serves 6

There are as many varieties of coleslaw as there are shades of pink, especially in the South! A lot of coleslaw recipes have sugar as an ingredient, but this one gets that bit of sweetness from sweet salad pickles, which don't mask the fresh flavors of the cabbage and carrots. We serve this every Fourth of July with Barbecued Pork Ribs (page 84) and Easy Baked Beans (page 133).

From Gwen:
The sweetest cabbage I've ever had was brought to us by friends from Spruce Pine, North Carolina.

1 firm head green cabbage, about 2 pounds

1 large carrot, peeled

½ small sweet onion, such as Vidalia, peeled and chopped fine

¼ cup diced salad pickles

½ cup mayonnaise

½ teaspoon salt

Pinch of black pepper

Remove and discard any bruised or undesirable outside leaves from the head of cabbage. Quarter the cabbage and grate it into a large bowl using the coarse side of a hand grater or the shredding blade of a food processor. Grate the carrot and add it to the cabbage, tossing together to combine. Add the onion, pickles, mayonnaise, salt, and pepper. Stir together until thoroughly mixed. Chill for 1 hour before serving.

Pink Salad

We always made this to take to Family Night suppers at church. Its official name was Congealed Fruit Salad, but it was known at our house as pink salad, because, well, it's pink! Besides, anything with the word *congealed* in the title just sounds gross to me, and this is anything but.

Serves 8

1   cup boiling water

1   3-ounce package strawberry-flavored gelatin

1   3-ounce package cream cheese, room temperature

1   15-ounce can crushed unsweetened pineapple, drained

2   ripe but firm bananas, peeled and diced

1   6–ounce jar maraschino cherries with juice, stems removed

½   cup chopped pecans

1   cup heavy cream

From Gwen: Substituting orange-flavored gelatin gives this salad a soft, appealing peach color.

Pour the boiling water into a large mixing bowl. Add the gelatin and stir until dissolved. Blend in the cream cheese, stirring until it is thoroughly mixed and the gelatin is completely dissolved. Cool in the refrigerator until the mixture thickens but is not fully gelled, about 45 minutes. Add the pineapple, bananas, cherries, and nuts, and mix gently.

In a separate bowl, use an electric mixer or whisk to beat the cream until stiff. Gently fold the whipped cream into the thickened gelatin mixture, and pour into a 6 x 9 x 2-inch dish. Refrigerate overnight, or until firm.

Lettuce Wedge Salad with Trisha's Easy Thousand Island Dressing

Serves 4

From Trisha: This dressing also makes a great topping for burgers.

From Gwen: There are no pickles in the dressing, thus no "islands." I call it Rushin' Dressing because you can mix it quickly when you are rushing to get dinner on the table.

I'm the hick who always asks the uptown restaurant waiter if they have Thousand Island dressing. They usually give me that look (you know the one), then politely inform me it is not on the menu. I know there are lots of wonderful dressings out there, and I've sampled most of them, but I always come back to this one. I usually whip it up and pour it over a big iceberg lettuce wedge.

- 1 head iceberg lettuce
- ½ cup mayonnaise
- 3 tablespoons ketchup
  Dash of Tabasco sauce
  Dash of black pepper

Wash the lettuce and remove any damaged or wilted outer leaves. Remove the lettuce core and discard. Cut the head into quarters and set it aside.

In a medium bowl, whisk together the mayonnaise and the ketchup. Add the Tabasco sauce and pepper to taste. Place a lettuce wedge on each serving plate. Drizzle with the dressing.

Quick Lettuce Core Removal Tip

Slam the head of lettuce down on a cutting board, core-side down. The core will separate from the rest of the head with a twist and come out easily.

Minty Greek Salad

I am a big fan of Greek salads, but at restaurants I seem to find myself always picking the vegetables and cheese out of the lettuce. One day I thought, why make it with lettuce at all? This recipe is just veggies and feta. I love it!

Serves 4

- 2 cucumbers, peeled and cut into chunks
- 16 pitted green olives
- 16 pitted black olives, such as kalamata
- 24 grape tomatoes, halved
- 2 cups feta cheese, crumbled
- ¼ cup olive oil
- 2 tablespoons fresh lemon juice
  Pinch of salt and pepper
- 1 tablespoon fresh mint, chopped

In a large bowl, combine the cucumbers, olives, tomatoes, and feta cheese. In a small bowl, mix the olive oil and lemon juice. Pour the dressing mixture over the vegetables. Season with salt and pepper to taste. Garnish with the mint.

Broccoli Salad

Serves 10

This is great served with Barbecued Pork Ribs (page 84) or prepared to take to a covered dish supper, because it's sturdy enough to stand at room temperature for a while without wilting. It also adds great color to a picnic spread.

½ pound bacon

2 cups small broccoli florets

1 cup mayonnaise

1 tablespoon cider vinegar

⅓ cup chopped onion

¼ cup sugar

¾ cup raisins

½ cup sunflower kernels

From Beth: Low-fat mayonnaise can be substituted for regular without significantly changing the taste or texture.

In a medium skillet, cook the bacon over medium heat just until crisp; drain on paper towels. When cool enough to handle, crumble the bacon and set aside.

Bring a large saucepan of salted water to a boil. Add the broccoli and blanch until bright green and slightly softened, about 3 minutes. Drain well, run under cold water to stop the cooking, and drain again.

In a mixing bowl, combine the mayonnaise, vinegar, onion, sugar, and raisins. Add the broccoli and toss to coat with the dressing. Refrigerate for 1 hour.

Just before serving, fold in the sunflower kernels and all but 2 tablespoons of the crumbled bacon. Sprinkle the reserved bacon over the salad to garnish. Serve immediately.

Chicken Salad with Fruit

This unusual take on chicken salad is a meal in itself, with the rice, fruit, and almonds as well as cooked chicken. Just add bread or crackers.

5   boneless, skinless chicken breasts, cooked (see page 61)

1   cup mayonnaise

2   tablespoons olive oil

2   tablespoons orange juice

1   teaspoon salt

3   cups cooked rice, cooled

1½   cups green grapes, halved

1   13-ounce can pineapple tidbits in juice, drained

1   15-ounce can mandarin oranges, drained

1   cup slivered almonds

     Pepper

In a large bowl, stir together the mayonnaise, oil, orange juice, and salt. Dice the cooled chicken, then add to the dressing with the rice, grapes, pineapple, oranges, and almonds, folding gently to coat the ingredients with the dressing. Add pepper to taste and gently mix again.

Cover the bowl and refrigerate overnight to allow the flavors to develop. Serve chilled.

Trisha's Homemade Chicken Salad

I keep this chicken salad in the refrigerator pretty much year round. It's easy to make, and it keeps in the fridge for a week. Of course, at my house, it only lasts a few days! I serve this on toasted bread, or with wheat crackers as an appetizer.

6   medium boneless, skinless chicken breasts

½   teaspoon salt

4   hard-boiled eggs, peeled and diced

½   cup sweet pickle relish

1   cup mayonnaise

    Salt and pepper to taste

Place the chicken in a large pot with water to cover. Add the salt, bring to a boil, then reduce the heat to a low simmer and cook the chicken until tender, about 45 minutes (see Note). Drain the chicken, cover, and refrigerate until cool, or up to 24 hours.

Pull the cooled chicken into shreds and place in a large bowl. Add the eggs, relish, and mayonnaise, and stir together gently until well mixed. Season with salt and pepper.

Serves 10

From Gwen: It may sound weird, but I love this for breakfast on a slice of toasted bread!

Note: You may also cook the chicken in a pressure cooker, in which case you should reduce the cooking time to 15 minutes.

Margaret's Cranberry Salad

Serves 12

From Gwen:
A Monticello friend prepared this recipe at my request and gave it a big thumbs-up!

My sister Beth's sister-in-law, Margaret, makes this salad, and it's a nice alternative to plain cranberry sauce for holiday meals. In fact, it's rich enough to serve as a dessert!

1   13.5-ounce can crushed pineapple in juice

2   3-ounce packages lemon gelatin

7   ounces ginger ale

1   16-ounce can whole cranberry sauce

2   ounces Dream Whip, prepared (or 8 ounces Cool Whip)

1   8-ounce package cream cheese, room temperature

½   cup toasted pecans, chopped (see Note)

Note: To toast pecans, place them on a baking sheet. Place in a 350°F oven or toaster oven for 10 minutes, or until they are fragrant and golden brown.

Drain the pineapple and pour the juice into a measuring cup, reserving the pineapple separately. Add enough water to the pineapple juice to make 1 cup. Bring the liquid to a boil in a medium saucepan. Add the gelatin and stir until it dissolves. Chill the gelatin until it is cool but not set. Stir in the ginger ale and chill for 1 additional hour, or until partially set.

Combine the cranberry sauce and the reserved pineapple and add to the gelatin mixture. Pour into a 9 x 9 x 2-inch dish and refrigerate until firm, 4 hours or overnight. Prepare the Dream Whip according to package directions, and then blend in the softened cream cheese. Spread the cheese mixture over the gelatin salad like frosting, then sprinkle with the chopped pecans.

Spinach Salad with Garlic Dressing

I'm not a cooked spinach fan, but I do like spinach served fresh in a salad. (And I love any salad that has bacon as an ingredient!) I'm also not a mushroom gal, so I leave those out when I make it, but it's good either way.

½   pound bacon

¾   cup olive oil

¼   cup red wine vinegar

½   teaspoon salt

1   teaspoon minced garlic

     Freshly ground pepper

1   pound leaf spinach, tough stems removed

½   pound mushrooms, thinly sliced

In a medium skillet, cook the bacon over medium-high heat until just crisp. Drain on paper towels and, when cool enough to handle, crumble. Set aside.

In a small bowl, whisk together the oil, vinegar, salt, garlic, and pepper. Chill and beat vigorously before using.

Wash the spinach leaves very well and spin dry. Tear the leaves into small pieces and place in a medium salad bowl. Add the mushrooms and bacon and toss to combine. Pour ⅔ cup of the dressing over the salad (reserve the rest for another use) and toss again. Serve immediately.

Serves 6

From Beth: My friend Venita shared this recipe with me. It's a special-occasion kind of salad.

From Gwen: I've tasted many of Venita's recipes. She's a natural when it comes to southern cooking!

Sweet and Crunchy Garden Salad

Serves 4 to 6

From Beth: Draining and chilling the mandarin oranges in advance will keep them from breaking apart when you toss the salad.

Browning the almonds in sugar gives a great sweet crunch to this salad. I have to state for the record that this is one of the best salads I've ever tasted.

- 1 cup sliced or slivered almonds
- ½ cup sugar
- 1 head iceberg lettuce, rinsed
- 1 head romaine lettuce, rinsed
- 1 cup vegetable oil
- ¼ cup red wine vinegar
- 1 tablespoon chopped fresh parsley
- 1 teaspoon salt
- Dash of black pepper
- Dash of cayenne
- 3 green onion (scallion) tops, thinly sliced
- 1 22-ounce can mandarin oranges, drained and chilled

Mix the almonds with ¼ cup of the sugar in a medium saucepan. Cook over medium heat, stirring as the sugar melts and the almonds brown. Carefully spread the almonds on an ungreased baking sheet to cool, using a metal spatula; the nuts will be very hot. When completely cooled, break the candied almonds into tiny pieces.

Tear the iceberg and romaine lettuce into pieces and wash well. Dry the greens thoroughly and transfer them to a salad bowl. Cover and refrigerate if not serving immediately.

Combine the oil, vinegar, remaining ¼ cup sugar, and the parsley, salt, pepper, and cayenne in a bowl, and mix well. Chill covered, in the refrigerator, until ready to serve.

Combine the lettuce, sliced green onions, candied almonds, and orange segments in a large salad bowl. Just before serving, toss the salad with enough dressing to coat the greens.

From Gwen: Seeing is believing! This salad is consumed rapidly even by self-professed salad haters!

Mexican Salad

Serves 12

From Beth:
This is a fun dish for children to help with.

What's great about this salad is that it only involves opening a few cans and layering the veggies with shredded cheese. It's simple, healthy, and looks pretty in a glass bowl to boot!

1 15-ounce can black beans, drained and rinsed

1 15-ounce can diced tomatoes with green chiles, drained

1 15-ounce can whole kernel corn, drained

1 8-ounce jar chopped, pickled jalapeños, drained

2 cups shredded Cheddar cheese

2 tablespoons chopped fresh cilantro (optional)

1 lime, cut in wedges

1 large bag corn chips (I like the scoop-type chips for this)

In a large bowl, combine the beans, tomatoes, corn, and jalapeños, and mix well.

Spread one-third of the bean mixture in the bottom of a large serving bowl. Sprinkle with one-half of the grated cheese. Top with half of the remaining bean mixture, and all but ¼ cup of the remaining cheese. Finish with a final layer of the bean mixture and garnish with the reserved ¼ cup cheese and the chopped cilantro. Serve with lime wedges and chips for scooping up the salad.

Trisha's Pasta Salad (The Original)

Like most families, we struggle to get enough vegetables into our diets. This pasta salad, served cool, is full of great greens and reds, and it is so tasty! The sunflower kernels give it a nice crunch.

Serves 6

12 ounces rotini pasta

5 ounces Cheddar cheese, grated

2 tablespoons olive oil

2 tomatoes, diced

2 broccoli florets, blanched

1 bell pepper, seeded and diced

Salt and pepper to taste

½ cup salted, roasted sunflower kernels

Bring a large saucepan of salted water to a boil. Add the pasta and cook for 9 minutes, or until it is tender; you don't want it too al dente. Drain the pasta and transfer it to a mixing bowl. When the pasta has cooled to room temperature, add the cheese, olive oil, tomatoes, broccoli, and bell pepper, and mix well. Season with salt and pepper and mix again. Top with the sunflower kernels.

Garth's Pasta Salad

Garth has to claim this recipe because he modified my basic pasta salad to suit his tastes and changed it completely! He likes to eat it warm because he loves the way the cheese melts into the other ingredients, so he doesn't wait for the pasta to cool down at all. He also says the secret to making the tomatoes taste so good is salting them separately. Who knew he was Gartha Stewart?

- 12 ounces rotini pasta
- 12 ounces spinach tortellini
- 2 dozen grape tomatoes, sliced in halves
- 1 teaspoon salt
- ½ teaspoon pepper
- 10 ounces Cheddar cheese, shredded
- 3 tablespoons olive oil

In a large saucepan, cook the rotini and tortellini for 10 minutes, or until they are at a desired tenderness. Drain the noodles. In a small bowl, toss the sliced tomatoes with the salt and pepper. While the pasta is still warm, toss it with the tomatoes, cheese, and olive oil. Serve warm.

beef and pork

Most of the meat dishes cooked in my family were made using ground beef, because it was inexpensive and readily available. When I was six years old, my parents moved us from town to a 30-acre farm just outside the city limits where we had a huge garden and also raised our own beef. After that, I remember we had steak a lot more often! You won't find a recipe for grilling steak in this cookbook, because my daddy always said a great steak is one that was cut properly and had just the right amount of fat on it before you laid it on the grill; all it needed was salt and pepper. When I would break out the Heinz 57 at the table (still my steak sauce of choice), he would say that any sauce at all ruined a good steak!

In the South, pork is most often used for barbecue, but my mother also made it lots of other tasty ways. When I was a child, getting really juicy pork chops from the grocery store was easy. Hogs are raised to be leaner these days, so be sure when you're shopping to pick a thicker-cut pork chop or loin if you can. I recommend at least a 1-inch-thick cut for pork chops and 1½ inches to 2 inches for stuffed pork chops. If you start out with a great piece of pork, whether it be ham, ribs, roast, or chops, your meal will taste better, no matter what the recipe.

Roast Beef with Gravy

Roast beef is all about Sunday afternoons after church for me. Mama would get up early and put the roast on to cook, then turn off the oven when we left for church and let it sit until we got home again. The memory of walking through the door and smelling that amazing aroma still makes my mouth water! The hardest part about this meal was waiting for the gravy to be made before you could sit down to eat it!

I've never been a fan of canned gravies or gravy starters, so I don't usually make gravy unless I have drippings from roasting beef or turkey. I like the gravy on the roast and on the white rice I usually cook to go with dinner; Garth puts the gravy on everything!

1   5-pound boneless chuck roast

    Salt and black pepper to taste

1   large red onion, sliced

¼   cup cider vinegar

4   tablespoons all-purpose flour

Preheat the oven to 450°F.

Line a 9 x 13 x 2-inch pan or your oven's broiler pan with a sheet of heavy-duty aluminum foil large enough to fully wrap the roast. The shiny side of the foil should be up. Sprinkle the roast on all sides with salt and pepper and place it in the center of the foil. Spread the onion slices over the top of the roast and pour the vinegar around it. Bring the ends of the foil together and fold several times, then fold the ends together to completely enclose the roast. Pour about 1 inch water into the pan around the foil-wrapped roast. Bake for 3 to 4 hours, or until the meat is fork-tender and brown. Check the water level in the pan regularly during cooking and replenish it if necessary. If any juice seeps from the foil seals during roasting, save it to use in making the gravy.

When the roast is done, remove the package from the baking pan and let it cool for a few minutes. Open the package carefully to preserve all the juices and transfer the meat to a platter; cover with a tent of foil to keep it warm while you make the gravy.

Pour the roasting juices into a measuring cup and let the fat rise to the surface. Skim off the fat, reserving 4 tablespoons in a saucepan and discarding the rest. (If the fat measures less than 4 tablespoons, add enough butter to make up the difference.)

Measure the remaining defatted pan juices; if you have less than 2 cups, add water to make 2 cups.

Add the flour to the fat in the saucepan and stir with a wire whisk to make a roux. Cook over medium-low heat until the flour is lightly browned, about 1 minute. Slowly whisk in the reserved pan juices and stir until thickened.

Slice the roast or cut it into chunks (it will be very tender), and serve it with the gravy.

Gwen's Old-Fashioned Potato-Beef Casserole

Serves 6

My family likes casseroles because they get the whole meal in one pan, and this is a favorite. It was probably born as a result of my mom's trying to put food on the table on a budget, and while a lot of people cook with ground beef because it is relatively inexpensive, I would pay big bucks to get to eat this every now and then! This is similar to a shepherd's pie, but a bit heartier, I think.

From Gwen: Potatoes cook quickly. Test often for tenderness and don't overcook them.

3   pounds white or red potatoes, peeled and sliced ¼-inch thick

1   pound lean ground beef

½   cup chopped onion

4   tablespoons (½ stick) butter

¼   cup flour

1   teaspoon salt

¼   teaspoon black pepper

2   cups milk

2   cups grated sharp Cheddar cheese

½   cup unseasoned dry bread crumbs

Place the potatoes in a large saucepan with water to cover by 1 inch. Add a generous pinch of salt and cook for 15 minutes, or until tender. Alternatively, cook the potatoes in a pressure cooker for 5 minutes, releasing the pressure immediately to prevent overcooking. Drain the potatoes and arrange them in a 6 x 9 x 2-inch casserole dish.

In a large skillet, combine the beef and onion and cook together over medium heat until the beef is browned and the onion softened, 12 to 15 minutes. Pour off the excess fat.

Preheat the oven to 350°F.

Melt the butter in a medium saucepan and whisk in the flour to make a roux. Cook over medium heat, whisking constantly, until the mixture bubbles and the flour turns light brown in color. Gradually whisk in the milk and continue to stir while cooking over medium heat. When the mixture thickens, whisk in the salt and pepper, then stir in the cheese and browned beef.

Pour the ground beef mixture over the potatoes and bake the casserole for 20 minutes until heated through and bubbling. Sprinkle the bread crumbs on top of the casserole and bake until the crumbs are toasted, about 5 minutes longer.

Note: Because all the ingredients are fully cooked, if they are still hot when you assemble the casserole, the baking time can be greatly reduced or even eliminated; simply brown the crumb topping under the broiler for a couple of minutes.

Daddy and Mama, 2005.

Ribbon Meatloaf

I love homemade biscuits, and I love meatloaf, so it's no surprise I'm pretty fond of this recipe. The sauce is so terrific, especially poured over that wonderful homemade biscuit dough with a little ground beef rolled inside. Yum!

1	pound lean ground beef
1	tablespoon minced onion
1½	teaspoons salt
½	teaspoon pepper
⅓	cup self-rising flour (see Note)
2	cups canned tomatoes, drained and juices reserved
1¾	cups frozen peas, thawed
1	recipe biscuit dough (page 151)

From Gwen:
This is one time it's okay to knead extra flour into the biscuit dough recipe to make it easier to roll and cut.

Combine the beef, onion, salt, and pepper in a large skillet and cook over medium heat until the meat is browned, 12 to 15 minutes. Remove from the heat. Stir in the flour and ⅓ cup of the reserved tomato liquid. Remove 1 cup of this meat mixture and set aside. Add the tomatoes, crushing them with your hands as you add them, and the peas to the skillet. Set aside.

Preheat the oven to 450°F.

Note: If you do not have self-rising flour, substitute ⅓ cup regular flour, ½ teaspoon baking powder, and a pinch of salt.

On a well-floured surface, roll the biscuit dough into a large rectangle about ½ inch thick. Spread the reserved cup of meat mixture thinly over the dough, then roll the dough like a jelly roll, beginning from one long edge. Place the roll on a greased baking sheet. Using kitchen shears or a very sharp knife, cut 1-inch slices almost through to the bottom of the roll. To expose some of the filling, pull alternate slices to the left and right. Bake for 15 minutes, or until browned.

Reheat the beef and vegetable mixture. Slice the baked loaf and spoon some of the hot vegetable and meat mixture over each slice.

Meatloaf

Serves 8 to 10

I probably make meatloaf once a week, and I've developed some pretty strong opinions about what works and what doesn't. I have sampled meatloaf across the country, and when it's good, it's usually because it's a simple rendition. If I don't like it, it's usually because someone tried to get fancy with it and put something in it that didn't belong there! This is the one I make most often. I prefer to use lean ground beef because it keeps the meatloaf from being too moist. Also, be sure to remove the meatloaf from the pan as soon as it's done; otherwise, the fat that has rendered into the pan will be absorbed back into the meat—not good!

From Trisha: If you've never had a cold meatloaf sandwich the next day, you don't know what you're missing.

- 2 pounds lean ground beef
- 20 saltine crackers, crumbled
- 1 large egg, lightly beaten
- ¼ cup ketchup
- 1 tablespoon yellow mustard
- 1 teaspoon salt
- ½ teaspoon pepper
- 1 medium onion, finely chopped

Preheat the oven to 350°F.

Gently mix the beef, cracker crumbs, egg, ketchup, mustard, salt, pepper, and onion until blended. Shape the mixture into two loaves and place side by side crosswise in a 9 x 13 x 2-inch pan. Bake the loaves for 1 hour, or until they are browned. Transfer to a platter immediately and allow the loaves to cool slightly and firm up before slicing.

Creamed Beef

Serves 4

This is one of those old-fashioned dishes that people either love or hate. I *love* creamed beef on toast. In fact, it's what I have for breakfast on my birthday every year! In our house, this dish is affectionately known by another name I can't print in this cookbook, but whatever you choose to call it, it's yummy!

1   pound lean ground beef

¼   cup all-purpose flour

2   cups milk

1½   teaspoons salt

¼   teaspoon pepper

4   bread slices, toasted and cut in half diagonally

Sauté the beef in a large skillet over medium heat, breaking it up with a wooden spoon and cooking until it is no longer pink, 12 to 15 minutes. Drain off the excess fat and sprinkle the meat with the flour (see Note). Stir and cook the beef and flour over medium heat until the flour has completely coated the beef and cooked slightly. Stir in the milk and continue to cook until the mixture becomes smooth and thickens, about 8 minutes. Add the salt and pepper. Serve over toast triangles.

From Gwen: This recipe is traditionally made with salted chipped beef from a jar, but I found my family preferred the lightly salted flavor of very lean ground beef. Put a pat of real butter on top before serving.

Note: If you use very lean beef, there will be just enough fat to mix with the flour without draining the excess fat.

Pork Chops and Rice

Serves 6

Sometimes it's nice to make a meal that takes only a couple of steps to get into the oven, and then you can forget about it for an hour while it cooks. The beef broth gives the rice a great flavor. I serve this with Cooked-to-Death Green Beans (page 130).

4	tablespoons butter
1	cup long-grain white rice
6	pork chops, bone in
	Salt to taste
1	10-ounce can beef broth
¾	cup water
6	onion slices, separated into rings
¼	teaspoon pepper

Preheat the oven to 350°F.

In a medium skillet, melt the butter over medium-low heat. Add the rice and sauté until it is light brown, about 5 minutes.

Spread the rice in 9 x 13 x 2-inch casserole. Season the pork chops with the salt and arrange them on top of the rice. Pour the broth and water over the chops. Spread the onion rings over the chops and sprinkle with the pepper. Cover the dish with aluminum foil and bake for 45 minutes, or until the pork chops are tender. Remove the pork chops to a plate and keep warm, then cover the dish and return the rice to the oven for an additional 15 minutes. If the rice is dry, add a bit more water before returning it to the oven. Serve the pork chops on a bed of the rice.

Stuffed Pork Chops

This dish takes a bit of attention, but the results are well worth the effort for a special meal. The steam that rises from the water in the bottom of the pan keeps the pork chops tender and moist. Mom used canning jar rings instead of a rack to elevate the chops above the water.

- 3 tablespoons butter
- 1 medium onion, finely chopped
- 2 tablespoons chopped fresh parsley
- ½ cup bread crumbs
- 1 teaspoon salt
- ¼ teaspoon pepper
- ⅛ teaspoon garlic powder
- 1 large egg, lightly beaten
- 4 bone-in pork chops, about 1½ inches thick, with pockets
- 1 cup all-purpose flour
- ¼ cup vegetable oil

Preheat the oven to 325°F.

Melt the butter in a large skillet over medium-high heat. Add the onions and sauté until they are translucent, about 7 minutes. Remove the pan from heat and stir in the parsley, bread crumbs, salt, pepper, and garlic powder. Stir in the beaten egg.

If your pork chops don't have pockets cut into them, insert the point of a small sharp knife horizontally into the fat-covered edge. Move the knife back and forth to create a deep pocket about 1½ inches wide.

Fill the pocket of each chop with the bread crumb mixture. Secure the openings with toothpicks and cotton thread or twine.

Dredge the stuffed chops lightly in flour, shaking off the excess. Wipe out the skillet used previously in making the stuffing and place over medium-high heat. Add the oil and, when hot, add the chops. Sear over medium heat until lightly browned, about 3 minutes on each side.

Put water in the bottom of a roasting pan with a rack, being careful not to cover the rack with water. Place the chops on the rack and cover the roaster with the lid or aluminum foil. Bake the chops for 1 hour, then uncover and continue baking for 20 minutes longer, to crisp the surface a bit.

Barbecued Pork Ribs

Serves 8

Since moving to Oklahoma, I have noticed that a lot of the barbecue there is made with beef. I started making these Georgia pork ribs a couple of years ago for the Fourth of July, and they quickly became tradition around here. Cut the racks into two-rib portions and serve them with Easy Baked Beans (page 133) and Fourth of July Coleslaw (page 54) for an awesome holiday feast!

From Gwen:
These take some extra time and effort, but it really pays off! Hint: The marinade can really bake onto the pan during cooking. Using a baking bag makes cleanup a lot easier.

- 2 cups soy sauce
- 1 cup water
- ½ cup light brown sugar, packed
- 1 tablespoon dark molasses
- 1 teaspoon salt
- 5 pounds meaty pork ribs

Marinade

- ⅓ cup water
- 1 14-ounce bottle ketchup
- 1 12-ounce bottle chili sauce
- ½ cup light brown sugar, packed
- 1 teaspoon dry mustard

In a medium saucepan, combine the soy sauce, water, ½ cup brown sugar, molasses, and salt. Bring the marinade to a boil and set aside to cool.

Put the ribs in a large, turkey-size oven baking bag or sealable plastic bag. Support the bag in a 12 x 14-inch baking pan. Pour the marinade over the ribs and seal the bag. Marinate the ribs in the refrigerator overnight, turning the bag occasionally to thoroughly coat the meat.

The next day, preheat the oven to 375°F.

Drain and discard the marinade from the bag. Cut 4 slits in the top of the baking bag if you are using one. Otherwise, drain the marinade, transfer the ribs to the baking pan, and cover the pan with foil. Bake the ribs for 2 hours.

While the ribs are baking, prepare the barbecue sauce. In a large saucepan, blend the water, ketchup, chili sauce, brown sugar, and dry mustard. Bring this mixture to a boil, stir well to dissolve the sugar, and set aside to cool.

When the ribs are cooked and tender, open the bag and discard the drippings. Lower the oven temperature to 350°F.

Brush the ribs on both sides with the barbecue sauce and return them to the oven to bake for 30 minutes longer. Just before serving, throw the ribs onto the barbecue or blacken them under the broiler to give them a bit of a char.

Pork Barbecue Sauce

Makes
1½ quarts

I respect people who won't share old family recipes, but when I find something good, I want everybody to be able to make it for themselves, and that's how I feel about my daddy's barbecue sauce. I truly believe Daddy could have bottled and sold this sauce, it was so popular! It's a personal preference, but I like a thin, vinegar-based barbecue sauce instead of the thick, ketchup-based sauces.

From Gwen:
Use this on chopped, sliced, or pulled pork.

- 1 small onion, ground fine
- 1 quart cider vinegar
- 12 ounces tomato juice
- 1 tablespoon pepper
- 1 tablespoon sugar

Chop the onion finely and purée it in a blender with ½ cup water. Place the puréed onion in a 2-quart saucepan with additional water to cover. Bring to a boil, and reduce the heat. Cook, stirring constantly, until the water has almost evaporated. Add the vinegar, tomato juice, and pepper, and mix well. Bring to a boil, and then stir in the sugar. Immediately remove from the heat to cool and store. Serve with your favorite barbecue dish.

Gwen on her childhood farm in Willacoochee, Georgia, 1958.

Pork Roast with Sauerkraut

Even those who say "No!" to sauerkraut will love this specialty dish from family friend Betty Maxwell.

Serves 8 to 10

- 2 pounds sauerkraut, undrained
- 1 4-pound Boston butt pork roast
- ½ cup packed light brown sugar

Preheat the oven to 375°F.

Spread the sauerkraut and its liquid in the bottom of a 10 x 12 x 3-inch roasting pan. Push the pork roast down into the sauerkraut and sprinkle with the brown sugar.

Cover the pan and bake for 1 hour and 30 minutes, or until the roast registers 170°F on a meat thermometer. Remove the meat to a platter and spoon the drained sauerkraut around the roast.

From Gwen: Betty loves to cook but doesn't like to eat alone. (Who does?) I'm fortunate to be on her invitee list!

Baked Ham with Brown Sugar Honey Glaze

Serves 20 to 30

From Gwen:
If you don't want or need a whole ham, you can bake half a ham, but choose the butt (meatier) end rather than the shank end.

This is the main attraction of our traditional Easter meal, and we think those spiral-sliced prebasted hams take a backseat to our version. Ask your butcher to order a whole smoked water-added ham such as Gwaltney, Hamilton, or Smithfield, and have him remove and quarter the hock. This not only makes the ham fit more easily into your pan but also gives you the hock pieces to use another time and contribute unbeatable seasoning to soups and veggies. Serve with Potato Salad (page 53) and Baby Lima Beans (page 132).

18–20-pound smoked ham, water added, ham hock removed

1   16-ounce box light brown sugar

1   cup (8-ounce jar) clover honey

Adjust the oven racks to accommodate a large covered roasting pan. Fit the pan with a shallow rack. Preheat the oven to 350°F.

Unwrap the ham and rinse it in cold water. Place it on the rack in the roasting pan. Cover the pan with the lid and open the vents in the lid slightly to allow steam to escape. Bake the ham for half the estimated cooking time. (Total cooking time is about 20 minutes per pound.) Halfway through the estimated cooking time, in a separate saucepan, mix the sugar and honey until smooth. Pour the mixture over the ham. Continue baking the ham, basting occasionally with the drippings in the roaster.

Check for doneness at the end of the estimated cooking time by inserting a meat thermometer at a meaty point (not into fat or touching the bone). It should register 160°F.

Allow the ham to stand for 15 minutes before slicing to allow the juices to set.

Breakfast Sausage Casserole

You see this recipe a lot in the South. It's great because you do all the work the night before; the next morning, this wonderful meal bakes while you're having a nice, leisurely cup of coffee! Beth makes this on Christmas Eve so it can bake Christmas morning during the present-opening frenzy.

Serves 12

6   slices white loaf bread

1   pound fresh bulk pork sausage with sage

10 ounces sharp Cheddar cheese, grated

5   large eggs, lightly beaten

2   cups half-and-half

1   teaspoon salt

1   teaspoon dry mustard

From Gwen: Jack always requested grits with this breakfast.

Cut the bread into 1-inch cubes and spread in the bottom of a greased 9 x 12 x 2-inch casserole.

In a medium skillet, brown the sausage over medium heat until fully cooked and no longer pink. Drain off and discard the rendered fat. Spread the cooked sausage over the bread and top with the cheese. Stir together the eggs, half-and-half, salt, and dry mustard. Pour this mixture over the cheese. Cover the casserole with aluminum foil and refrigerate for 8 hours or overnight.

The next day, preheat the oven to 350°F.

Bake the covered casserole for 50 minutes, or until set and slightly golden. Remove from the oven and allow the casserole to set for 15 minutes before serving.

poultry, fish, and pasta

I remember one diet I went on several years ago that included grilled chicken at just about every meal. To this day, I have difficulty eating plain grilled chicken, and I'm always looking for ways to make chicken interesting. These dishes give you every choice: basic southern fried chicken, a leaner, baked "fried" chicken in cornflake crumbs, and everything in between.

I've included only a few fish recipes in this cookbook, mainly because I'm just not a fan of fishy-tasting recipes. But I know it's good for you, and I'm trying to eat more of it. Growing up in middle Georgia certainly dictated the kinds of fish we ate; the only salmon we ate came out of a can, and the only fresh fish we ate was the fish we caught ourselves. You can't beat a day filled with baiting your own hook (or asking Daddy to handle the icky worms!) and catching your own dinner.

I also didn't grow up eating much pasta, though it's one of my passions now. For the most part, I believe in leaving pasta dishes to the professionals, but a few dishes have become mainstays for me. You don't have to be Italian to serve a flavorful spaghetti sauce with your plain old spaghetti noodles, and I would put my fettucine Alfredo up against any version you can find!

Chicken Baked in Cornflake Crumbs

Serves 4 to 6

From Gwen:
To make crumbs, place cornflakes in a sturdy resealable plastic bag and roll over the sealed bag with a rolling pin. Remove the chicken skin for less fat.

This is a nice recipe for southern girls like me who love fried chicken but realize they can't eat it everyday. The cornflakes give you that crispy crust like fried chicken without all of the added fat of deep-frying—not that I'm saying there's a thing wrong with deep-frying! My motto is "Everything in moderation, including moderation."

2–3 shakes of Tabasco sauce (optional)
   1 cup buttermilk, well shaken
   1 cup cornflake crumbs
   8 chicken pieces (drumsticks, thighs, breasts), with skin
   1 teaspoon salt
  ¼ teaspoon pepper

Preheat the oven to 350°F.

Line a cookie sheet with aluminum foil and spray the foil with cooking spray. Shake the Tabasco sauce into the buttermilk and pour into a shallow bowl. Place the cornflake crumbs in another bowl or on a piece of waxed paper. Dip each piece of chicken in the buttermilk, and then roll it in the crumbs. Place the coated chicken pieces on the cookie sheet and sprinkle with the salt and pepper.

Bake the chicken for 1 hour, or until the crust is golden brown and the thigh meat is no longer pink at the bone. Check this with the point of a sharp knife. Remove the pieces from the pan and serve while the chicken is warm.

Gwen's Fried Chicken with Milk Gravy

My biggest complaint about fried chicken is that all of the flavor ends up on the outside, and the meat is usually bland. Not my mama's! The secret is in the prep. When you soak the chicken overnight in salt brine, the salt infuses into the meat and makes it so tasty! When I asked my mom how long to fry the chicken, she said, "Just cook it 'til it sounds right." I have since fried enough chicken to completely understand this sentence, but at the time— you can imagine! As chicken begins to fry, it's loud because of all the water cooking out into the fat. It gets quieter as it gets done. Who knew? Now you do!

Serves 4 to 6

From Gwen: Milk makes the gravy rich and smooth.

- 8 serving pieces of chicken, light or dark meat
- 2 tablespoons salt
- 2 cups peanut oil
- 1 teaspoon black pepper
- 2 cups all-purpose flour

Milk Gravy
- 4 tablespoons oil
- 4 tablespoons all-purpose flour
- 2 cups milk
-   Salt and pepper to taste

Put the chicken pieces in a large bowl and cover them with water. Sprinkle the salt in the water, cover the bowl, and refrigerate for 4 hours or overnight.

Pour oil into an electric frying pan or deep, heavy skillet to a depth of 1 inch. Heat the oil to 375°F. (Check the temperature by sprinkling flour over the oil. If the flour sizzles, the oil is hot enough.)

continued . . .

Drain the water from the chicken, sprinkle each piece with pepper, and coat the pieces with flour. Carefully place the chicken in the hot oil. Place the cover on the pan and open the vent to allow a small amount of steam to escape. Cook for 15 minutes. Remove the cover and, using tongs, turn each piece of chicken. Replace the cover and cook for 15 minutes more, or until done. Use a sharp, thin-bladed knife to check for doneness by slicing a drumstick to the bone. Neither the meat nor the juices should be pink. Drain the chicken on paper towels and keep warm while you make the gravy.

Pour off all but 4 tablespoons of the oil from the pan in which the chicken was fried, leaving the bits of browned flour in the pan. Sprinkle in the 4 tablespoons flour. Stirring with a wire whisk, cook the flour and drippings until the flour is browned, about 1 minute. Slowly stir in the milk and cook until the gravy thickens, 5 to 10 minutes. Season with salt and pepper.

Pass the chicken and gravy separately.

Barbecued Chicken

Serves 6

As a young man, my dad worked with the State of Georgia Extension Service, where he learned to barbecue chickens by the hundreds. Over the years, he cooked thousands of chickens that were sold on the town square, at football games, or horse shows. He and his friends would build a huge pit with cement blocks and top them with specially made racks that could hold about 50 chicken halves each. To turn the chickens, another rack was placed on top, and two men, one on each end of the racks, would flip the entire rack at once! My mom has adapted Dad's recipe to serve a family, not the whole town.

3   2½-pound frying chickens, split (see Note)

4   tablespoons salt

1   cup cider vinegar

¾   cup peanut oil

1   teaspoon Tabasco sauce

⅛   teaspoon black pepper

¼   cup water

1   teaspoon cayenne pepper

Daddy with Bank of Monticello grill.

Put the chicken halves in a very large bowl or deep pot and cover with water. Sprinkle 3 tablespoons of the salt in the water. Cover the bowl or pot and refrigerate the chickens in this brine for 6 hours or overnight.

Prepare a fire in a grill with the grilling rack set 16 inches above the coals (see Note).

In a saucepan, mix together the vinegar, remaining tablespoon salt, peanut oil, Tabasco sauce, black pepper,

¼ cup water, and the cayenne. Bring this mixture to a boil, stir well, and remove from the heat.

When the coals are uniformly covered with gray ash, spread them in a single layer. Drain the chicken, pat dry, and place the halves on the grill, skin side up. Baste with the sauce and cook for 30 minutes. Using tongs, turn the chickens skin side down and baste the top with sauce. Continue to grill the chickens for an additional 1½ hours, turning and basting the chicken every 15 minutes. Add charcoal as needed to maintain a hot layer of coals. Check for doneness by twisting a drumstick. It should move easily.

Note: If you cannot find small chickens, use larger ones (3–3½ pounds) and quarter them. If the grill rack cannot be adjusted, cook the chickens closer to the coals and turn the halves more often to avoid burning.

Chicken Pie

Comfort food. That's all I've got to say!

- 3 cups cooked, shredded chicken
- 2 cups chicken broth
- 1 10-ounce can cream of chicken soup
- 1 cup self-rising flour (see Note)
- ½ teaspoon pepper
- ½ cup (1 stick) butter, melted
- 1 cup buttermilk, well shaken

Preheat the oven to 425°F.

Put the chicken in a 2-quart casserole dish. Combine the broth and soup in a medium saucepan and bring the mixture to a boil. Pour the broth mixture over the chicken.

In a separate medium bowl, mix the flour with the pepper. Stir in the melted butter and the buttermilk. Pour this mixture over the casserole and smooth the top; do not stir. Bake the casserole for 45 minutes, or until the crust is brown and the filling beneath is hot and bubbly.

Serves 6

From Beth:
This is chicken potpie without the pot! Hold the veggies.

Note: If you don't have self-rising flour, you may substitute 1 cup all-purpose flour, 1½ teaspoons baking powder, and ½ teaspoon salt.

Chicken Broccoli Casserole

Serves 10

This casserole is hearty and contains everything you could want on the table in one dish. It's a favorite of our whole family. It makes ten servings, but my husband likes it cold for breakfast the next day, so in my house you'd better take your serving at dinner the night before, 'cause that's all you're gonna get!

- 2 cups cooked rice
- 3 cups cooked chopped broccoli
- 1 cup sour cream
- ½ cup mayonnaise
- 1 tablespoon lemon juice
- 1 10-ounce can condensed cream of chicken soup
- 10 ounces Cheddar cheese, grated
- ½ teaspoon salt
- ¼ teaspoon pepper
- 4 chicken breasts, cooked and shredded (see page 61)

Preheat the oven to 350°F. Grease a 9 x 13 x 2-inch baking dish with butter or nonstick cooking spray.

Spread the rice in an even layer in the baking dish. Make a second layer with the broccoli.

In a large bowl, mix the sour cream, mayonnaise, lemon juice, condensed soup, half of the grated cheese, and the salt, pepper, and chicken. Pour this mixture over the broccoli and top with the remaining grated cheese. Bake for 40 minutes.

Let stand for 5 minutes before serving.

No-Baste, No-Bother Roasted Turkey

Serves 20 to 25

From Gwen: This turkey is tender and produces lots of pan juices for the gravy.

Every Thanksgiving, I hear cooks groaning about having been up all night basting the big turkey, and I just smile. I've found a foolproof, easy way to make a great turkey and get your sleep too! It also makes the most tender, moist turkey I've ever tasted. The first time I cooked Thanksgiving dinner for my family, Garth couldn't believe this method would actually work, so he politely asked me to cook a "stunt" turkey so he could taste it for himself before the big day. Most of my friends have been just as hesitant, but once they have tried it my way, they never go back to the old way. To make sure the oven temperature doesn't drop too quickly, I put a sign on it threatening bodily harm to anyone who even thinks about opening the oven door during this process!

1   12-pound turkey, completely thawed, all giblets removed

½   cup (1 stick) salted butter, softened

2   tablespoons salt

2   teaspoons pepper

2   stalks celery, cut in lengths to fit turkey cavity

1   medium sweet onion, such as Vidalia, cut in half

1   large carrot

2   cups boiling water

Adjust the oven racks so the covered roasting pan fits easily inside the oven. Preheat the oven to 500°F.

Rub the butter on the outside and in the cavity of the turkey. A self-basting turkey will not require all of the butter. Sprinkle the salt and pepper on the inside and on the outside of the turkey. Put the celery, onion, and carrot in the cavity. Place the turkey, breast side up, in a large roasting pan. Pour the boiling water into the pan. Cover with a tight-fitting lid and put the pan in the preheated oven.

Start a timer when the oven temperature returns to 500°F. Bake for exactly 1 hour and turn off the oven. Do not open the oven door. Leave the turkey in the oven until the oven cools; this may take 4 to 6 hours. Reserve the pan juices and refrigerate the turkey if it will not be served soon after roasting.

Serve with Grandma Lizzie's Cornbread Dressing (page 145) and Giblet Gravy (recipe follows).

Daddy holding a wild turkey.

Giblet Gravy

Makes 2 cups

From Gwen:
Give it a try!
Giblets are
people, too!

For some people, it just isn't Thanksgiving without giblet gravy for the turkey and potatoes. Mom has included directions for a giblet-free version for those of us who have seen a giblet and never want to eat one!

Giblets and neck from turkey (see Note)

1 teaspoon salt, plus more to taste

4 tablespoons fat skimmed from the turkey roasting pan

4 tablespoons all-purpose flour

2 cups turkey broth

2 large eggs, hard-boiled, peeled, and chopped fine

Pepper to taste

Place the giblets in a saucepan with 3 cups water and 1 teaspoon salt. Bring to a boil, then reduce the heat, skim off any foam that rises to the surface, and simmer until tender, about 25 minutes. Cool the giblets in the cooking liquid. When cool, strain the broth into a measuring cup; if it is less than 2 cups, add chicken stock to make a full 2 cups. Pull the meat off the bones and shred the giblets. Cover and reserve.

In a medium saucepan, mix the flour with the skimmed fat and cook until the roux is lightly browned, about 3 minutes. Slowly whisk the turkey broth into the roux and cook until the gravy thickens. Stir in the shredded giblets and chopped eggs. Season to taste.

Note: There are those, Trisha included, who pass on the giblet gravy because they don't care for giblets, which traditionally include the liver, heart, gizzard, and the dark meat from the neck. For giblet-free gravy, substitute a bit of shredded white meat from the turkey or boiled and shredded chicken breasts for the giblets.

Baked Orange Roughy

This recipe is a nice alternative to fried fish, and the spices give the fish plenty of flavor. You can substitute any mild fish for the roughy.

Serves 6

From Gwen: Choose only the freshest fish. If you are in an area where fresh fish isn't readily available, use frozen.

- 2 cups dry bread crumbs
- ½ cup grated Parmesan cheese
- ½ cup chopped fresh parsley
- 1 teaspoon paprika
- ½ teaspoon dried oregano
- ¼ teaspoon dried basil
- 2 teaspoons salt
- ½ teaspoon pepper
- 6 orange roughy fillets, 3–4 ounces each
- 1 cup buttermilk, well shaken
- Lemon wedges, for serving

Preheat the oven to 375°F.

In a large, flat dish, mix the bread crumbs, cheese, parsley, paprika, oregano, basil, salt, and pepper. Spray a 9 x 13 x 2-inch baking dish with cooking spray. Dip each fillet in the buttermilk, and then coat it with crumbs, pressing to be sure they adhere. Arrange the fillets in the baking dish and bake uncovered for 25 minutes, or until the fish flakes easily with a fork. Serve with the lemon wedges.

Herb's Fried Catfish

Serves 12

From Gwen: Our family attended many fish fries held outdoors on the banks of Herb's pond in Jasper County, Georgia. His wife, Glenda, loves to fish, and she provided most of the fish.

From Trisha: You can make the hushpuppies in the same oil as the fish, but let it cool down to 250°F first.

Growing up, I was lucky to have a catfish pond just down the hill on our farm. My daddy had created the pond from a natural spring when I was a little girl and stocked it with catfish and bream. We had many a wonderful fish fry with freshly caught catfish from our pond all through my childhood. Fresh fried fish served with Mama's Cornmeal Hushpuppies (page 140)—you couldn't ask for a better meal! My only suggestion is that you let someone else dress the catfish. Yuck!

 6 pounds catfish fillets, cut into 2-inch strips

 3 tablespoons plus ½ teaspoon salt

 1 cup self-rising cornmeal

 1 cup cracker meal

 ½ teaspoon pepper

 4 tablespoons Cajun seasoning

 1½ gallons peanut oil

In a large bowl, prepare a salt-water brine by combining 3 tablespoons salt with 2 quarts water. Add the fish and more water if needed to just cover the fish. Soak the fish in the brine for 30 minutes.

Mix the cornmeal, cracker meal, remaining ½ teaspoon salt, pepper, and Cajun seasoning in a 1-gallon plastic bag.

In a large (3-gallon) catfish cooker or deep Dutch oven, heat the oil to 350°F. Preheat the oven to 150°F.

Coat the fish by shaking a few pieces at a time in the plastic bag with the crumbs.

Opposite: Mama, the great fisherman . . . um, woman! (1960)

Drop 8 to 10 of the coated fish fillets into the hot oil. Cook until the coating is light brown; the fillets will cook quickly, in less than 5 minutes. Pieces will float to the top of the oil when they're done. Drain the cooked fish on paper towels and keep warm in the oven while you fry additional batches. Let the oil return to 350°F before adding and cooking more fish.

Salmon Croquettes with Creamed Peas

Makes 30 croquettes

From Gwen: Forget the creamed peas where Trisha's dad was concerned. Pass the creamed potatoes!

Note: If you like, substitute ¾ pound shrimp, cooked, shelled, and chopped, or 14 ounces tuna for the salmon in this recipe.

Cooking fish is not one of my specialties, but I do love this recipe because it doesn't taste fishy. I think it was probably my mom's attempt to get us girls to eat some fish by disguising it in fried bread crumbs. What can I say? It worked. The creamed peas give the croquettes a slightly sweet accent. This topping tastes good on other meats too, like baked chicken and ham.

- 3 tablespoons butter
- 2 tablespoons finely chopped onion
- ⅓ cup all-purpose flour
- ½ cup milk
- 2 teaspoons fresh lemon juice
- ¼ teaspoon salt

  Dash of pepper
- 1 14-ounce can pink salmon, drained (see Note)
- 1 cup fine dry bread crumbs
- 2 large eggs, beaten

Creamed Peas
- 2 pounds fresh green peas, shelled
- 3 tablespoons salted butter
- 2 tablespoons all-purpose flour
- 2 cups milk
- 1 teaspoon salt
- ¼ teaspoon pepper

- 3 cups peanut oil, for frying

Melt the butter in a medium skillet over medium-high heat. Add the onion and sauté until softened, about 3 minutes. Use a wire whisk to stir in the flour. Cook for 1 minute, and then stir in the milk. Cook until the mixture is very thick, stirring constantly for 1 minute. Remove from the heat and add the lemon juice, salt, and pepper.

Allow the white sauce to cool slightly, and then stir in the salmon. Shape the mixture into small balls or cones about 1½ inches in diameter. Place the bread crumbs in a shallow dish. Mix the beaten eggs with ¼ cup water. Double-coat the croquettes by rolling them first in the crumbs, then in the egg mixture, and then in the crumbs again. Place each coated croquette on a baking sheet. Cover the croquettes and set them aside.

To make the creamed peas: Bring 1 cup lightly salted water to a boil. Add the peas and cook for 6 to 7 minutes, or until tender. Drain and set aside. Melt the butter in a medium saucepan over medium heat.

Stir in the flour and cook until smooth and lightly browned, about 1 minute. Slowly whisk in the milk and continue cooking on medium heat, stirring often. Add the salt and pepper. Cook until the mixture is smooth and thick, about 6 minutes. Stir in the cooked peas and keep warm while you fry the croquettes.

Heat the oil to 375°F in a deep, heavy pot. Preheat the oven to 150°F.

Add about 12 croquettes at a time to the hot oil and cook until they are golden brown. Drain the croquettes on paper towels and keep them warm in the oven as you fry the remaining croquettes. Make sure the oil returns to 375°F before adding and cooking more croquettes, or they will be heavy and greasy.

Black Bean Lasagne

Everybody has a tried and true basic lasagne recipe, but occasionally it's nice to try something different. Somewhere along the way, I decided to replace the meat with beans, and the result was a hit. This lasagne keeps well in the refrigerator, and if you have leftovers, they freeze well. When I was single and living in Nashville, I would cool this lasagne and freeze portions in individual freezer bags. It was perfect to pull one out of the freezer in the morning before I went to work in the studio, then microwave it for a minute or two when I got home in the evening.

1   16-ounce can diced or stewed tomatoes

1   12-ounce can tomato paste

2   teaspoons salt

½   teaspoon black pepper

¼   teaspoon garlic powder

1   tablespoon dried oregano leaves

1   small onion, finely chopped

8   ounces lasagna noodles

2   15-ounce cans black beans, rinsed and drained

1   16-ounce container ricotta cheese

16   ounces Cheddar cheese, shredded

16   ounces mozzarella cheese, shredded

In a large saucepan, combine the tomatoes and their juices, the tomato paste, 2 cups water, and the salt, pepper, garlic powder, oregano, and onion. Bring to a boil over medium-high heat, then reduce the heat and simmer, uncovered, for 30 minutes.

Meanwhile, bring a large pot of salted water to a boil. Add the lasagna noodles and cook according to package directions. Drain the noodles well and spread them on a baking sheet to prevent them from sticking together.

Preheat the oven to 375°F.

Spread 1 cup of the prepared sauce in a 9 x 13 x 2-inch baking pan. Make three layers each of noodles, sauce, black beans, ricotta, Cheddar, and mozzarella, ending with mozzarella. Bake for 40 minutes, uncovered. Allow the dish to stand for 15 minutes before cutting into squares and serving.

Fettuccine Alfredo

Serves 6

From Trisha:
If you try this recipe, make sure you don't have to drive afterward. Maybe it should come with a warning not to operate heavy machinery after eating!

I *love* pasta—and who doesn't? Because I didn't grow up cooking Italian food, I usually save my Italian experiences for my favorite Italian restaurants, like La Mela in the heart of New York's Little Italy and Anna's in Los Angeles. But a gal's gotta make fettuccine Alfredo occasionally. This is the very first home-cooked meal I tried on Garth, and I'm surprised he ever allowed me to cook for him again! It was early on in our relationship, and I wanted to impress him with my cooking skills, so I thought this recipe would be perfect. It is so rich it makes you full fast. That particular night, however, my Alfredo sauce came out so thick it was almost impossible to serve it from the pan. Garth, being the gentleman he is, took a big serving and attempted to eat it. I don't know if he finished it all, but it was so rich and filling he almost fell asleep in his plate! He says he has no memory at all from about halfway through the meal until he woke up hours later on the couch.

- 12   ounces fettuccine noodles
- ¾   cup (1½ sticks) butter
- 1   cup whipping cream
- ¼   teaspoon white pepper
- 2   cups freshly grated Parmesan cheese
- 1   teaspoon cornstarch
- 2   tablespoons snipped fresh chives or parsley

Bring a large pot of salted water to a boil. Add the pasta and cook according to the package directions.

In the meantime, make the sauce. In a medium saucepan over low heat, melt the butter. Whisk in the whipping cream and pepper, stirring frequently, until the mixture thickens slightly, about 5 minutes. Gradually stir in 1¼ cups of the Parmesan cheese. Cook and stir just until the cheese is melted. Whisk in the cornstarch and stir until slightly thickened, about 3 minutes.

Drain the pasta and add the hot noodles to the cheese mixture. Toss until the pasta is well coated. Transfer individual servings of the pasta to plates. Sprinkle 2 tablespoons Parmesan cheese over each serving, and garnish with the chopped chives or parsley.

Spaghetti with Meat Sauce

Serves 4 to 6

I am allergic to canned spaghetti sauce! Well, maybe not *really*, but I just can't eat spaghetti sauce out of a can or jar. This sauce is easy, and it is even better warmed over the next day, after the flavors have had a chance to settle in.

1	pound lean ground beef
¾	cup finely chopped onion
2	teaspoons minced garlic
2	16-ounce cans crushed tomatoes
2	6-ounce cans tomato paste
1½	teaspoons dried oregano
1	teaspoon salt
½	teaspoon pepper
2	1-pound packages spaghetti

Put the ground beef, onion, and garlic in a medium saucepan and cook together over medium-high heat until the beef is browned and the onions are softened, about 10 minutes. Add the tomatoes and their juices, the tomato paste, 1 cup water, and the oregano, salt, and pepper. Simmer uncovered, stirring occasionally, for 1 hour.

While the sauce simmers, bring a large pot of salted water to a boil. Add the spaghetti and cook until al dente, about 8 minutes, or according to package directions. Drain well and divide among plates. Spoon the sauce over the spaghetti and serve.

Baked Macaroni and Cheese

My mom made this cheese sauce when I was a child, mostly to pour over vegetables she was trying to get us to eat. I was a grown woman before I realized that steamed broccoli didn't have to be served with cheese sauce! It does make this homemade mac and cheese taste amazingly good, though!

- 2 teaspoons salt
- 1 pound elbow macaroni

Cheese Sauce
- 4 tablespoons (½ stick) butter
- 4 tablespoons all-purpose flour
- 1 teaspoon salt
- 2 cups milk
- 2 cups grated sharp Cheddar cheese

Topping
- ½ cup bread crumbs
- ¼ cup (½ stick) butter, melted

Preheat the oven to 350°F. Butter a 2-quart casserole dish.

Bring 4 quarts of water to a boil in a large saucepan. Add 2 teaspoons of salt and the macaroni. Bring the water back to a boil and cook the macaroni for 12 minutes, or until tender. Drain well.

Make the sauce while the macaroni cooks. Melt the butter in a 1-quart saucepan. Using a wire whisk, stir in the flour and 1 teaspoon of salt, stirring and cooking over medium heat until the roux bubbles and the flour turns pale brown, about 3 minutes. Remove the pan

continued . . .

from the heat and slowly whisk in 1 cup of the milk. Return the pan to the heat and whisk in the remaining 1 cup milk. Continue to cook, stirring constantly, until the sauce thickens. Add the cheese and stir until it melts.

Add the drained macaroni to the cheese sauce and mix thoroughly. In a small bowl, stir the bread crumbs together with the melted butter until the crumbs are moistened. Transfer the macaroni and cheese to the prepared baking dish, top with the buttered bread crumbs, and bake for 15 minutes, or until the dish bubbles around the edges.

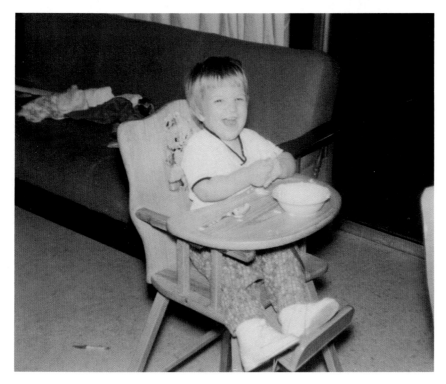

Me, showing an early love of food at age one.

sides

Once you've decided what entrée you're cooking for supper, the next step is figuring out what goes along with it. In this section you'll find plenty of healthy, colorful side dishes to expand your repertoire—maybe a few will become your stand-bys, as they are mine. You'll also find a really basic how-to on cooking fresh vegetables, like green beans. It's not hard to do—unless you've never done it before and have no idea how—so we show you. Many of these recipes have been made for so many generations in my family they were never written down; coming up with exact amounts involved trying something, making changes, and trying again. In general, when it comes to vegetables, we've taken the less-is-more approach, especially with seasonings like salt. It's always easier to add salt at the table than it is to take salt out of the finished dish! And while we've mentioned which entrées we typically serve with these side dishes, you should feel free to serve what you like with the entrées you like.

Betty's Cabbage Medley

Growing up in a classic meat-and-potatoes family, I can't remember a meal that didn't include meat. As an adult, I've learned you don't always have to have meat at dinner. This dish is a perfect choice for a meal that is all veggies and will leave you full and satisfied.

From Gwen: Get your veggie vitamins in one quick and pretty dish.

- 1 cup sliced carrots, ¼-inch rounds
- 1 cup thinly sliced onion
- 1 cup diced celery
- 1 small head cabbage, cut in chunks (about 6 cups)
- 1 tablespoon sugar
- 2 cups warm water
- ¼ cup corn oil

In a large heavy saucepan with a tight-fitting lid, arrange the vegetables in layers in the following order: Spread the carrots on the bottom of the pan, then top with the onions, celery, and cabbage. Sprinkle the sugar on top, and then pour in the warm water and oil. Cover the pan tightly and cook over high heat for 10 minutes, or until the vegetables are done but still crunchy. Remove the lid, stir the vegetables, then replace the lid and let the vegetables stand for 20 minutes, or until you are ready to serve.

Sautéed Cabbage

It's hard for families on the go to eat enough vegetables, so we decided to have one night every week that is only veggies. When we do, I always make this recipe. As the cabbage cooks, it sweetens a bit. I like to let it brown a little in the pan because I like the crispness and the flavor. Try it!

1 large head cabbage

3 tablespoons olive oil

3 tablespoons water (optional; see Note)

Salt and pepper to taste

Note: The cabbage will steam in its own juice. If the low setting on your stove is not low enough, add water to prevent scorching.

Peel off and discard any bruised or wilted leaves from the cabbage, and use a sharp knife to remove the core. Cut the head in half lengthwise, then cut the halves crosswise into thin shreds.

In a large skillet or saucepan, heat the oil and sauté the shredded cabbage over medium-high heat for 5 minutes, tossing and stirring often until wilted. Reduce the heat to very low, cover the pan with a tight-fitting lid, and cook for 30 minutes, or until the cabbage is tender. Stir frequently, as the cabbage can scorch easily. Season the cabbage with salt and pepper to taste.

Roasted Carrots

Here's another dish that's a hit on veggie night!

½   cup (1 stick) butter, melted

1   teaspoon salt

½   teaspoon pepper

2   pounds carrots, peeled and cut diagonally into 3 x ½-inch sticks

2   tablespoons chopped fresh dill or parsley (optional)

Preheat the oven to 400°F. Line a large jelly roll pan with aluminum foil.

In a medium bowl, mix the melted butter, salt, and pepper. Spread the carrots on the jelly roll pan and pour the butter mixture over them, stirring to coat. Roast for 25 to 30 minutes or until tender, stirring once. Toss with the chopped herbs, if using, and serve.

Serves 6

From Beth:
Try this same treatment on fresh asparagus. It's good!

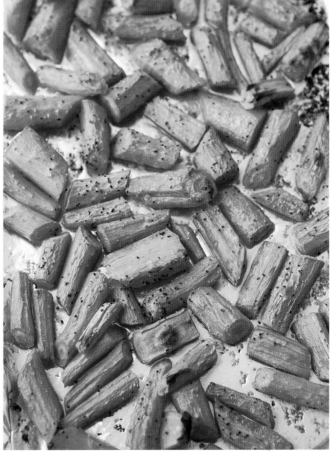

Zucchini Sauté

When Beth first made this very simple zucchini dish (which she created for our parents), Daddy asked, "Honey, how'd you learn to cook?" I thought that was funny because I think what he was really wondering was how she'd learned to cook something that Mama didn't make at home!

Serves 8

1	tablespoon olive oil
½	teaspoon minced garlic
4	zucchini squash, thinly sliced
½	teaspoon salt
¼	teaspoon pepper
¼	cup grated Parmesan cheese

Heat the olive oil in a medium skillet over medium heat. When hot, add the garlic and sauté for 2 minutes, or until fragrant; don't let it brown. Add the squash, salt, and pepper and cook until the squash is tender but still slightly crisp, about 5 minutes. Transfer the squash to a serving dish and sprinkle with the Parmesan cheese.

Collards

Serves 6

From Gwen:
I cook and freeze these for Trisha every summer.

I could live on collard greens and corn bread! I like collard greens better than turnip greens because I think collards are sweeter. When I make my corn bread and greens bowl (crumbled-up buttermilk corn bread covered with collard greens and a little juice), I add a little hot pepper just for fun. In the South, collard juice, or the cooking liquid that accumulates, is often called *pot likker*. My daddy always planted a big collard patch every spring, not only for the family but also to share with friends. Through the years, friends knew the patch was just out back of the barn and they were free to drive in and help themselves.

2   large bunches collards, homegrown or from the produce section

½   pound cured ham hock or salt pork

½   cup salt, for brine (optional; see below)

Daddy with a collard plant.

Prepare the collards for cooking by cutting the large stems from the center of the leaves. Wash the leaves thoroughly. If the collards are homegrown, soak the leaves briefly in a salt-water brine made by adding ½ cup salt to enough water to cover the leaves. Rinse well to rid the leaves of any insects. Stack and roll the leaves and cut them crosswise into 1-inch strips.

Put 2 inches of water in a saucepan large enough to hold the raw collards (the leaves can be pushed down tightly and will wilt to about one-quarter volume as they cook). Add the ham hock or pork and bring the water to a boil. Add the collards and toss with tongs until the water returns to a boil and the leaves wilt down into the pan. Reduce the heat, cover, and simmer over low heat for 1 hour, or until tender. Stir occasionally, checking to be sure there is enough liquid to prevent scorching. Taste the liquid and add salt if needed. Serve with Buttermilk Cornbread (page 154).

Fresh Green Beans (a.k.a. Tom Cruise Green Beans)

Serves 4

Garth and the girls and I went to Colorado one spring break and spent the week in the guesthouse of some friends. We skied all day and came home exhausted in the evenings. Our friends provided a chef for us, and it was great to come back to the cabin after a long day to a beautifully prepared meal. I had always made Cooked-to-Death Green Beans, but the chef made these green beans one night and we fell in love with them. (The girls also fell in love with the chef, who looked a little bit like Tom Cruise.) When we have veggie night, the girls always ask, "Are we having Tom Cruise?" You can imagine the looks we get from guests who've never been to our house on veggie night!

2   pounds fresh green beans, tips removed

4   tablespoons butter, melted

     Salt to taste

Wash and drain the beans. Put 1 cup water in a medium saucepan. Add the beans and cook until tender but still very crisp, about 6 minutes.

Drain the beans and add the butter, tossing to coat as it melts. Season with salt to taste.

Cooked-to-Death Green Beans

Serves 4

Note: Salt pork or Goya Ham-Flavored Seasoning may be substituted for the ham hock.

I make this with our home-canned green beans, but canned green beans from your grocery store cook down nicely with a little help from a ham hock. The recipe says to cook these for 30 minutes. I would really say just to cook them to death, but 30 minutes sounds sweeter.

2 quarts home-canned green beans or canned Blue Lake variety, with their liquid

½ pound cured ham hock (see Note)

Put the beans, their liquid, and the ham in a large, heavy saucepan. Cook, uncovered, on medium heat for 30 minutes. The beans are ready when the liquid has cooked down.

Cream-Style Corn

In the country, we planted a large garden every spring. It never seemed like a chore to shell peas or shuck corn because I always knew how good they were going to taste when they were cooked! If you've never had homemade cream-style corn, you don't know what you're missing. We always had a huge corn crop, so we made a lot of creamed corn and froze it in quart containers to enjoy year round. The kind of fresh corn you use can determine the thickness of the cooked dish. If it's too thick, add a little water. If it's too thin, add a little cornstarch.

12 ears fresh sweet corn, such as Truckers' Favorite or Merritt

4 tablespoons (½ stick) butter

Salt to taste

Shuck the corn and remove all the silks. Wash and drain the corn. Shave just the tips of the kernels using a very sharp knife or vegetable peeler. Cut away from you, allowing the tips to fall into a large bowl. Using the back of the knife, scrape the creamy juice from the kernels into the same bowl.

Melt the butter in a skillet over medium heat and add the corn. Cook the creamed corn for 20 minutes, stirring often, until thickened. Add water if the mixture becomes too thick. Season with salt to taste.

Serves 6

From Gwen:
Be sure you use juicy corn for this; otherwise, you won't get the right creamy texture.

If fresh creamed corn is a favorite, you might want to think about purchasing a corn cutter, which removes the tips and juice with one motion. You can order one online at www.homesteadharvest.com.

Baby Lima Beans

Serves 4

From Gwen: Trisha *loves* these beans!

We call these *butterbeans* in Georgia. I serve them with Baked Ham with Brown Sugar Honey Glaze (page 88) and Potato Salad (page 53). In college I had a friend named Tina, who is from Mississippi. When I would go home with her for the weekend, she would put mayonnaise in her butterbeans. Don't try this at home, because you will love it and it's more added fat that none of us need! (Okay, try it once!)

2 pounds baby lima beans, fresh in the shell, or 1 10-ounce package, frozen

2 tablespoons butter

½ teaspoon salt

¼ teaspoon coarse ground pepper

Shell the beans and wash thoroughly. Put 2 cups water and the salt in a medium saucepan and add the beans. Cook the beans for 30 minutes, or until tender. Drain the liquid and add the butter. Sprinkle lightly with black pepper before serving.

Easy Baked Beans

I serve baked beans with everything from hot dogs to Barbecued Chicken (page 96). They are a great side dish, and the bacon, molasses, and brown sugar in this version make them irresistible (see photo page 118).

Serves 10

1   pound bacon

1   large onion, such as Vidalia, finely chopped

4   15-ounce cans pork and beans

½   cup dark molasses

¼   cup light brown sugar, packed

2   tablespoons prepared yellow mustard

Preheat the oven to 350°F.

Fry the bacon in a large skillet over medium-high heat until crisp. Remove the bacon from the pan, leaving the drippings, and drain it on paper towels. Crumble and set aside.

Pour out and discard all but 4 tablespoons of the bacon drippings. Add the onion to the pan and sauté until softened, about 7 minutes. Stir in the beans, molasses, sugar, mustard, and bacon, and mix well.

Pour the beans into a 3-quart casserole and bake, uncovered, for 45 minutes.

Uncle Wilson's Baked Onions

Serves 12

From Gwen: My brother, Wilson, loves to cook. His baked onions can be served with anything but are especially good with Barbecued Pork Ribs (page 84) and Baked Ham with Brown Sugar Honey Glaze (page 88).

Note: Cook onions on the grill by sealing the packets more securely. Cover the grill and check for tenderness after 1 hour of cooking.

If you have access to real Vidalia onions, by all means use them here. Onions from Vidalia, Georgia, are the sweetest onions on the face of the earth! (But how do I really feel about them?) My uncle Wilson made these onions one Fourth of July, and they were a huge hit.

6 large sweet white onions, such as Vidalia

12 strips bacon

2 tablespoons butter

Preheat the oven to 350°F.

Peel and wash the onions. With the point of a small, sharp knife, cut a 1-inch core from the top of each onion. Wrap 2 slices of bacon around each onion, securing it with toothpicks, and put 1 teaspoon butter in each core. Place each onion on a square of aluminum foil and bring the edges loosely together at the top. Put the foil-wrapped onions in a large pan and bake for 1 hour and 20 minutes, or until the onions are tender when pierced with the tip of a knife. Cool the onions for a few minutes, then unwrap and cut in quarters to serve.

Steamed Yellow Squash

Serves 6

Cook out as much liquid as you can by uncovering and stirring often. A little browning doesn't hurt. You know, I don't even *like* squash, but this sounds yummy to me!

  4 tablespoons (½ stick) butter

  1 small sweet onion, such as Vidalia, peeled and finely chopped

 12 medium yellow crookneck squash, trimmed and sliced ¼-inch thick

 ½ teaspoon salt

 ¼ teaspoon pepper

Melt the butter in a large skillet over medium-high heat. Cook the onion in the butter until it browns slightly, about 5 minutes. Layer the squash slices into the skillet and sprinkle with the salt and pepper. Cover the pan, reduce the heat to low, and cook the squash for 20 minutes, or until tender. Remove the cover. Stir the squash and continue cooking until the liquid has cooked out, another 3 or 4 minutes.

Fried Okra

Serves 6

My daddy loved boiled okra, but it's too slimy for me. Fried okra, on the other hand, is great with everything!

- 12 tender okra pods, 4 inches or smaller
- ½ cup all-purpose flour
- 1 large egg, beaten
- ½ cup cornmeal
- ½ teaspoon salt
- 2 cups peanut oil

Wash the okra and trim the stem ends. Slice each pod crosswise into ½-inch rounds. Place the flour, egg, and cornmeal in separate shallow bowls. Coat the rounds with flour, then drop them into the beaten egg. Use a slotted spoon to transfer the okra rounds to the bowl with the cornmeal and toss to coat.

In a deep-fryer or large cast-iron Dutch oven, heat the oil to 350°F. Lift the okra out of the cornmeal, again using a slotted spoon, and shake off the excess cornmeal. Carefully drop the okra into the oil piece by piece so it doesn't stick together while cooking. Don't overcrowd the pan; you will need to cook 2 or 3 batches. Cook until light brown, about 15 minutes. Remove the cooked okra with a slotted spoon and drain on paper towels. Sprinkle with salt.

Garlic Grits Casserole

I think people who say they hate grits just haven't had them prepared correctly. Basic grits are pretty simple, and you can add what you like to make them tastier. My sister experimented with this flavorful herb and garlic cheese version for a yummy twist on an old southern favorite.

Serves 12

From Beth: Even non-grits-lovers should try this recipe from my mother-in-law, Blanche Bernard.

1	cup grits
4½	cups boiling water
1	teaspoon salt
10	ounces herb and garlic cheese, such as Boursin
¼	cup (½ stick) salted butter
2	medium eggs
½	cup milk
1	tablespoon salted butter, melted
1	cup crushed cornflakes

Preheat the oven to 350°F. Grease a 9 x 12 x 2-inch casserole dish.

Cook the grits in the boiling water with the salt until thickened, about 5 minutes. Add the garlic cheese and butter to the hot grits and stir until melted and incorporated. Beat the eggs and add the milk to the beaten eggs. Slowly stir the egg mixture into the grits. Pour the mixture into the prepared dish. Pour the melted butter over the cornflakes and stir to distribute the butter. Sprinkle the crumb mixture on top of the grits. Bake for 45 minutes.

Asparagus Casserole

Serves 8

This casserole belongs on a plate with roast beef, rice, and gravy for Sunday lunch. We probably didn't have it every Sunday, but it was often part of the standard after-church meal. I'm a little surprised that as children we ate asparagus, but Daddy always said we'd eat anything with Mama's cheese sauce on it!

From Gwen:
Using the liquid from the canned asparagus intensifies the flavor of the sauce.

4   tablespoons butter

4   tablespoons all-purpose flour

Asparagus liquid plus enough milk to equal 2 cups

½   teaspoon salt

5   ounces Cheddar cheese, grated

2   15-ounce cans asparagus spears, drained, liquid reserved

4   hard-boiled eggs, cracked and peeled

½   cup saltine cracker crumbs (about 10 crackers)

Preheat the oven to 350°F.

Melt the butter in a medium saucepan. Whisk in the flour to make a roux. Cook for 1 minute, and then whisk in the milk and the asparagus liquid. Add the salt and continue cooking until the sauce thickens, about 5 minutes. Add the grated cheese and stir until it's melted, about 1 minute.

From Beth:
You can substitute fresh asparagus for canned, but be sure to trim the tough ends and steam before using. Because you won't have any extra asparagus liquid from the can, use 2 cups milk.

Arrange the asparagus in the bottom of a 9 x 12 x 2-inch baking dish, alternating the stem ends so each serving includes both heads and stems. Thinly slice the eggs and arrange them over the asparagus. Pour the cheese sauce over the eggs and asparagus and sprinkle with the cracker crumbs. Bake the casserole for 20 minutes, or until it is lightly browned and bubbles appear around the edges.

Spanish Rice

I guess because most of my recipes are southern, we'll just have to say this one is way south of the border! This is a hearty side dish that can be used any time you serve rice. We serve this rice on the Fourth of July with Barbecued Pork Ribs (page 84).

Serves 8

From Gwen: Great with chicken, beef, or pork.

2 tablespoons butter

1 cup long-grain white rice

½ cup chopped onion

½ cup chopped green pepper

2½ cups canned tomatoes, diced or stewed

½ cup chopped pimiento

1 teaspoon salt

Dash of cayenne pepper

Tabasco sauce to taste

Preheat the oven to 375°F. Grease a 9 x 12 x 2-inch casserole dish

Melt the butter in a medium saucepan over medium-low heat. Add the rice, onion, and green pepper and sauté for 8 to 10 minutes, or until the rice is slightly browned and the vegetables are softened. Stir in the tomatoes, pimiento, salt, cayenne, and Tabasco. Transfer the rice to the prepared baking dish, cover tightly with aluminum foil, and bake for 30 minutes. Remove the dish from the oven, stir the rice, and check for tenderness. If the rice is tender but too soupy, cook another 5 minutes. If the rice is dry but not tender, add ½ cup water and return to the oven, covered, for another 5 minutes, or until the rice is done.

Mama's Cornmeal Hushpuppies

Makes 48

From Gwen:
The idea for adding jalapeños comes from Herb's sister, Patty.

Note: If you can't find self-rising cornmeal, substitute 2 cups cornmeal plus 3 teaspoons baking powder and ¼ teaspoon salt.

You can't have fried catfish without hushpuppies! Sometimes I add a few more jalapeños to the mixture for a little extra jolt.

There are several stories about how hushpuppies got their name. My favorite is the one where an old southern cook was frying them one day and heard her dog howling nearby, so she gave him a plateful and said, "Hush, puppy!" It might just be folklore, but I like it.

- 2 cups self-rising cornmeal (see Note)
- 1 large jalapeño, seeded and chopped fine
- ¾ cup finely chopped onion
- 2 cups buttermilk
- 8 cups peanut oil, for frying

In a large bowl, mix the cornmeal, jalapeño, and onion. Add enough of the buttermilk to make a stiff batter. You may not need the whole 2 cups.

Heat the peanut oil to 250°F. (If you are making these to serve with fried catfish, just let the oil cool until it reaches 250°F.)

Drop the batter into the hot oil by teaspoonfuls. The hushpuppies will turn over in the oil as they cook. They are done when they are brown all over, 4 to 5 minutes. Remove them from the oil with a slotted spoon and drain on paper towels. Keep the hushpuppies warm while you fry the remaining batter. Serve hot.

Home-Style French Fries

Serves 6

I'm not sure if I ever had a store-bought French fry before high school! Mama made these home fries and served them with fresh-off-the-grill burgers. They're the perfect side for Herb's Fried Catfish (page 106) and Mama's Cornmeal Hushpuppies (page 140).

6   medium white or red boiling potatoes

1   tablespoon salt

4   cups peanut oil

Peel the potatoes and slice them into ¼ x ¼-inch sticks. Put the sticks in a large bowl and cover with cold water. Sprinkle the salt into the water. Refrigerate the potato sticks in the salt water for 1 hour.

In a deep-fryer or cast-iron Dutch oven, heat the peanut oil to 375°F. Transfer half of the potatoes to a colander and drain thoroughly, leaving the rest in the cold water. Carefully drop the drained potatoes into the hot oil and fry until light brown, about 15 minutes. Using a slotted spoon, remove the potatoes to a paper towel–lined plate and sprinkle with additional salt while still hot, if desired. Bring the oil back to 375°F. Drain the remaining potato sticks and add to the oil. Keep the first batch of fries hot in a 150°F oven while you fry and drain the second batch. Serve piping hot.

Real Mashed Potatoes

Serves 6

If I had to name the dish that is requested most often at home it would be this one. My family will eat almost anything if they can have these whipped potatoes on the side! I have been asked many times what secret ingredient makes this recipe so good. The answer is—potatoes! You'll be amazed at how simple it is to make really great mashed potatoes. Everyone has his or her own preference, but I like to use red potatoes, as I think they are lighter and don't get gummy like other kinds can. I also peel the potatoes completely, leaving no trace of skin, but if you like the skins, simply leave them on. For this recipe alone, I would encourage everyone who doesn't have a pressure cooker to get one. They are safe and save a ton of time in the kitchen. A pressure cooker cuts the prep time for this recipe from 1 hour to 15 minutes.

5 pounds medium red-skinned potatoes

1 tablespoon salt, plus more to taste

½ cup (1 stick) butter, at room temperature

2 tablespoons milk

Pepper to taste

Peel the potatoes and cut them in 1-inch cubes. Place the potatoes and 1 tablespoon salt in a large saucepan with water to cover and bring to a boil. Reduce the heat and simmer the potatoes until very tender, about 30 minutes. (You can also cook the potatoes in a pressure cooker for about 5 minutes.)

Drain the potatoes and transfer them to a large mixing bowl. Add the butter, milk, and salt and pepper to taste. Use an electric mixer or a hand mixer to whip the potatoes to a smooth texture, about 5 minutes. You shouldn't see any lumps. If you do, keep mixing! Serve immediately.

Beth's Hash-Brown Potato Casserole

Serves 8

There are as many versions of this casserole as there are southern cooks and church cookbooks. Beth's is a compilation of several. I like the potatoes shredded instead of cubed and not as much butter as some recipes have (don't worry, there's still plenty!).

2	pounds large red potatoes, peeled
2	cups sour cream
10	ounces Cheddar cheese, shredded
1	10-ounce can cream of mushroom soup
1	small onion, finely chopped
1	teaspoon salt
½	teaspoon pepper
2	cups crushed Ritz crackers
½	cup (1 stick) butter, melted

From Beth:
If you're in a hurry, substitute a 2-pound bag of frozen hash browns, thawed, for the red potatoes.

Preheat the oven to 350°F. Grease a 9 x 13 x 2-inch casserole dish.

Use the large holes of a box grater or the grating blade of a food processor to shred the potatoes into a large bowl. Add the sour cream, cheese, soup, onion, salt, and pepper. Turn the mixture into the prepared baking dish and sprinkle with the crushed crackers. Pour the melted butter over the top of the casserole. Cover with foil and bake for 45 minutes, then uncover and bake for 20 minutes more, or until lightly browned on top.

Grandma Lizzie's Cornbread Dressing

Cornbread dressing is my absolute favorite part of the Thanksgiving meal. In fact, I have been known to make this recipe in July because I just can't bear the thought of eating it only once a year! The recipe was never written down until Beth and I demanded that Mama show us how to make it. She came up with the ingredient amounts and demonstrated the mixing technique. (Hint: You've gotta get your hands in it!)

Serves 12

½ loaf white bread, cut into small cubes and toasted

½ medium onion, finely chopped

2 tablespoons butter or turkey fat (skimmed from the pan drippings)

1 pound Buttermilk Cornbread (page 154; about ¾ recipe)

¼ pound saltine crackers (about 35 crackers or 1 sleeve), crumbled

3 hard-boiled large eggs, peeled and chopped

4 cups turkey pan juices (page 104), chicken broth (page 40), or low-sodium canned broth

Salt and pepper to taste

Preheat the oven to 350°F. Grease a 9 x 13 x 2-inch baking dish.

Place the bread cubes on a large baking sheet and toast in the oven for 30 minutes, turning once after 15 minutes, until lightly brown. Set aside to cool. Raise the oven temperature to 450°F.

In a medium skillet, sauté the onion in the butter until translucent and softened but not browned, about 5 minutes. In a very large bowl, crumble the corn bread, toasted bread cubes, and cracker crumbs. Add the onion and eggs and toss with a fork until mixed. Add 3 cups of the broth and mix well, adding more as needed to make a very moist but not soupy dressing. Season with salt and pepper to taste. Bake in the prepared pan for 15 minutes, or until lightly browned.

Sweet Potato Soufflé

This is a nice variation on regular sweet potatoes for a Thanksgiving side dish. It's almost a dessert, it's so sweet!

Serves 8

5 medium sweet potatoes (about 9 ounces each)

2 large eggs

1 cup granulated sugar

½ cup (1 stick) butter, at room temperature

1½ teaspoons vanilla extract

½ cup milk

Pinch of salt

Topping

1 cup finely chopped pecans

1 cup brown sugar, packed

⅓ cup all-purpose flour

¼ cup (½ stick) butter, softened

Preheat the oven to 400°F. Grease a 2½-quart baking dish with butter.

On a foil-covered baking sheet, bake the sweet potatoes for 1 hour, or until they are soft. When cool enough to handle, peel the potatoes, place the flesh in a large mixing bowl, and mash until very smooth. Add the eggs, sugar, butter, vanilla, milk, and salt. Combine well with an electric mixer or hand mixer. Turn the mixture into the baking dish.

In a medium bowl, stir together the pecans, brown sugar, flour, and butter until thoroughly combined. Spoon the mixture over the sweet potatoes, making an even layer. Bake the casserole for 30 minutes, or until slightly browned. Let the casserole sit for 5 minutes before serving.

quick breads and muffins

I could never be on a diet that eliminated an entire food group, and bread always seems to get the ax first in the diet world! I truly believe that moderation—not giving up something you love altogether—is the key. And bread is something I really do love!

This section includes the basic bread, muffins, corn bread, and sweet bread recipes I rely on year in, year out. Every single one of them is equally good toasted for breakfast, served warm with a little butter for a midafternoon snack with a cup of coffee, or any time you're hungry! And if you're like me, you'll be tempted to ignore the whole moderation thing and eat the entire loaf of Ashley's Banana Bread at one sitting.

Daddy's Biscuits

Biscuits are synonymous with southern cooking. If I had the time, I would have homemade biscuits at every single meal. They should be required in every household! When my niece Ashley was small, one of the things she liked best about going to Granddaddy and Grammy's house was breakfast. There was usually a conversation the night before about all the awesome things on the menu—bacon, grits, sausage, and, of course, homemade biscuits. Ashley would be up early to help make the biscuits, standing on a chair beside Granddaddy, wearing a big apron and covered with flour.

4 tablespoons vegetable shortening

2 cups self-rising flour (see Note)

¾ cup buttermilk, well shaken

Preheat the oven to 450°F. Lightly grease a baking sheet with non-stick cooking spray. Using a pastry blender or two table knives, cut the shortening into the flour until it resembles coarse meal. Use a fork to stir in the buttermilk to make a soft dough, or until the dough comes together and leaves the sides of the bowl. Continue stirring with the fork until all the flour is worked into the dough, then turn the dough out onto a lightly floured board and knead 3 or 4 times until smooth and manageable.

With your hands or a floured rolling pin, flatten the dough to a thickness of ½ inch. Cut the dough with a 2½-inch floured biscuit cutter. Place the rounds on the baking sheet 1 inch apart for crisp biscuits or almost touching for softer biscuits. Bake for 8 to 10 minutes, or until lightly browned.

Makes 12

From Gwen: I mix the dough from start to finish with my fingers. I taught Trisha's dad to use a fork because all the dough seemed to end up on his big hands and not in the pan!

From Trisha: Reroll dough scraps for an extra couple of biscuits.

Note: If you cannot find self-rising flour, substitute 2 cups all-purpose flour, 3 teaspoons baking powder, and ¼ teaspoon salt.

Jack's Yeast Bread

From Gwen:
Jack used specially shaped tubes such as stars, rounds, and scallops for party sandwich bread.

This was Daddy's "I quit smoking" bread. When I was in high school, he stopped smoking for good. Being a man who was never still, he started looking for ways to occupy his hands other than smoking. He bought some of the first bread flour ever to hit the shelves in Monticello, Georgia, and started experimenting. He became known around town for his homemade bread, and often made loaves for bake sales and church suppers.

- 2 cups whole milk
- 3 tablespoons solid shortening
- 2 tablespoons sugar
- 2½ teaspoons salt
- 1½ tablespoons active dry yeast
- ¼ cup lukewarm water (80° to 85°F)
- 5–6 cups bread flour
- ¼ cup butter, melted

Scald the milk and add the solid shortening, sugar, and salt. Stir until the shortening is melted, and cool to lukewarm (80° to 85°F).

In a large, warm bowl, sprinkle the yeast over the lukewarm water. Wait 5 minutes and stir the yeast into the water. Add the cooled milk mixture. Stir in enough flour to make a very stiff dough. Turn the dough out onto a lightly floured board and knead about 10 minutes, or until it is smooth and satiny.

Place the dough in a warm, lightly buttered bowl. Turn the dough to coat it with butter. Cover the bowl with a cloth and allow the dough to rise in a warm place (80° to 85°F), free from drafts, until the dough has doubled in bulk, about 2 hours.

Using your fingers or your fist, punch down the dough to release the air and turn the dough over in the bowl so the smooth oiled side is on top. Cover the bowl and let rise again until almost doubled in bulk, about 30 minutes.

Turn the dough out onto a board and divide into 2 equal portions. Shape each portion into a ball, cover with a cloth, and allow to rest for 10 minutes. Shape each ball into a loaf and place the loaves into 2 greased loaf pans, 5½ x 9½ x 3½-inches.

Brush the tops of the loaves with melted butter, cover, and let rise until doubled in bulk, about 1 hour. Preheat the oven to 400°F. Bake for 40 to 45 minutes. Turn the loaves out on a rack to cool. The bread is done when it sounds hollow when lightly tapped on the sides or bottom.

Note: Water may be substituted for part or all of the milk. Bread made with milk has a browner crust.

Daddy making yeast bread using Lizzie's bread tray.

Buttermilk Cornbread

Serves 8

This is great bread for any meal, but one of my favorite ways to eat it is crumbled up in a big bowl with really cold milk. Mmmm! Beth likes it cold with buttermilk. Now that's just wrong!

4 tablespoons corn oil or bacon drippings

3 cups self-rising cornmeal

2½–3 cups buttermilk, well shaken

Preheat the oven to 450°F.

Pour 2 tablespoons of the oil into a well-seasoned 9-inch cast-iron skillet (see Note) and place over medium-high heat. Put the corn-

meal in a large mixing bowl. Make a well in the cornmeal and add the remaining 2 tablespoons oil. With a fork, stir in enough of the buttermilk to make a batter that is thick but can be easily poured into the hot skillet. You may not need all 3 cups.

Carefully pour the batter into the skillet. The oil will come up around the edges. Use the back of a spoon to smooth this over the top of the batter. Continue to heat on the stovetop for 1 minute, and then transfer the skillet to the oven and bake the corn bread for 20 minutes, or until browned on top. Immediately turn the cornbread out onto a cooling rack to keep the crust crisp.

Note: Season a new cast-iron skillet by coating the inside with vegetable shortening (not butter) and heating the pan in a very hot oven (450°F) for 1 hour. Cool the skillet and wipe off any excess oil before using. To care for a seasoned skillet, wipe the interior after each use. Do not soak it in soapy water or put it in the dishwasher.

Ashley's Banana Bread

My sister hates bananas. Imagine all of the yummy recipes that eliminates for her! Nonetheless, when my niece Ashley makes this banana bread, it's so good, even Beth will eat it. Maybe it has something to do with all that butter.

¾ cup (1½ sticks) butter

1½ cups sugar

2 large eggs

4 ripe bananas, mashed

1 teaspoon vanilla extract

2 cups sifted all-purpose flour

1 teaspoon baking soda

1 teaspoon salt

½ cup buttermilk, well shaken

1 cup chopped pecans

Preheat the oven to 350°F. Grease 2 9 x 5-inch loaf pans.

With an electric mixer, cream the butter and sugar together until light and fluffy. Add the eggs one at a time, beating well after each addition. Beat in the bananas and vanilla. Sift the flour together with the baking soda and salt and add to the banana mixture alternately with the buttermilk, beginning and ending with flour. Fold in the nuts.

Pour the batter into the loaf pans and bake for 55 minutes. Cool slightly in the pan before turning the loaves out onto wire racks to cool completely.

Lemon Blueberry Bread

Serves 8

From Beth: Dusting the blueberries with flour before adding them to the batter keeps them from sinking to the bottom of the pan.

Every summer, my sister Beth fills her freezer with blueberries her family has picked. They eat as many as they can while the berries are in season, share some with friends and family, and then freeze the rest. This quick bread is good made with fresh or frozen blueberries, and Beth uses lemons from her own lemon tree, right in her backyard! (I'm jealous!)

1	cup fresh blueberries
1½	cups plus 2 tablespoons sifted all-purpose flour
⅓	cup butter, melted
1	cup granulated sugar
3	tablespoons fresh lemon juice
2	large eggs
1	teaspoon baking powder
1	teaspoon salt
½	cup milk
2	tablespoons grated lemon zest
½	cup chopped pecans

Glaze

2	tablespoons fresh lemon juice
¼	cup confectioners' sugar

Preheat oven to 350°F. Grease a 4 x 8 x 2-inch loaf pan.

In a medium bowl, toss the blueberries in 2 tablespoons flour and set aside. In the bowl of an electric mixer, beat together the butter, granulated sugar, 3 tablespoons lemon juice, and eggs. Sift together 1½ cups flour, the baking powder, and the salt. Add the flour and milk alternately to the butter mixture, beginning and ending with flour. Fold in the lemon zest, pecans, and blueberries. Pour the batter into the pan and bake for 1 hour and 10 minutes; a toothpick inserted in the center of the loaf should come out clean. Cool for 10 minutes in the pan, then turn out onto a wire rack.

Make the glaze by stirring together 2 tablespoons lemon juice with the confectioners' sugar until completely smooth. Drizzle over the top of the loaf while it is still warm, allowing the glaze to drip down the sides. Serve the loaf warm or at room temperature.

Blueberry Muffins

Makes 18

These are the best muffins of all time! My friend Lisa brings me quarts of fresh frozen blueberries every year, and I make these yummy muffins until the blueberries run out. Of course, either fresh or frozen blueberries will work in these muffins. This is a classic choice for breakfast; serve with a fresh cup of coffee.

2	cups all-purpose flour
¾	cup sugar
1	tablespoon baking powder
½	teaspoon salt
½	teaspoon ground cinnamon
½	cup (1 stick) butter, melted
½	cup milk
2	large eggs, beaten
½	teaspoon vanilla extract
1½	cups fresh blueberries

Preheat the oven to 350°F. Place paper liners in an 18-cup mini-muffin pan.

Sift the flour with the sugar, baking powder, salt, and cinnamon into a large bowl. Make a well in the center of the flour mixture. Add the melted butter, milk, eggs, and vanilla, and stir just enough to moisten the flour. Gently fold in the blueberries.

Spoon the batter into the lined muffin pan. Bake for 25 minutes, or until a toothpick inserted in a muffin comes out clean.

Pecan-Pie Muffins

These muffins are rich and chewy, but they are also a bit delicate, so be sure to use paper liners in the muffin tins and spray them with nonstick spray; otherwise, they will crumble when you peel off the liners. This recipe also makes great mini-muffins; just shorten the baking time by 5 minutes.

Makes 9

1   cup chopped pecans

1   cup brown sugar, packed

½   cup all-purpose flour

2   large eggs

⅔   cup (1⅓ sticks) butter, melted

Preheat the oven to 350°F. Place paper liners in 9 muffin cups and spray with nonstick cooking spray.

In a large bowl, combine the pecans, sugar, and flour. Make a well in the center of the mixture.

In a separate bowl, beat the eggs until foamy. Add the melted butter and stir to combine. Pour the egg mixture into the well in the dry ingredients, stirring just until moistened.

Spoon the batter into the cups, filling each two-thirds full. Bake the muffins for 20 minutes, or until a toothpick comes out clean when inserted in a muffin. Remove the muffins from the pans immediately and cool on wire racks.

cakes, pies, and puddings

I try to reserve my desserts for home-baked items so I can truly enjoy the flavors and can appreciate the hands that made them. When it's my hands that have done the baking, I'm always excited that I was able to make something that tasted so good!

I think one of the big reasons people don't cook much anymore is the misguided notion that it takes too much time and it's just too hard. If you learn one thing in this cookbook, I hope it is that good home-cooked food can be quick and easy. The cakes in this book range from super-easy, just throw it in the pan (Pineapple Upside-Down Cake) to good luck with that (Lizzie's Old-Fashioned Cocoa Cake with Caramel Frosting). If you're tackling one of the more difficult recipes, set aside a couple of hours to make it in advance, and rely on the quicker recipes or the quick substitution ideas for days when you don't have a lot of time to spend in the kitchen. The banana pudding recipe goes from start to finish literally in about 15 minutes!

Pies are a great dessert to make ahead because they store well for a day or two. I make a couple of pecan pies a few days before Thanksgiving every year. It's one less thing I have to think about on that hectic day, and it makes for a wonderful dessert whether served cold or warmed up in the microwave for a few seconds.

Sour Cream Coffee Cake

Serves 12

Beth makes this cake every time it's her turn to take refreshments for her Sunday School class. It's made in a bundt pan, so it looks beautiful, and the sour cream gives it great flavor and a moist texture. Those little tunnels of brown sugar and nuts are a nice surprise. People always ask her for the recipe.

1 cup (2 sticks) butter, room temperature

2 cups granulated sugar

2 large eggs

2 cups all-purpose flour

1 teaspoon baking powder

½ teaspoon salt

1 cup sour cream

1 teaspoon vanilla extract

Streusel Mixture

½ cup light brown sugar, packed

1½ teaspoons ground cinnamon

½ cup finely chopped pecans

Glaze

1 cup confectioners' sugar

1½ tablespoons milk

½ teaspoon vanilla extract

From Gwen:
Be sure to begin the layering with batter. Putting the streusel mixture first produces a sticky cake that is difficult to remove from the pan.

Preheat the oven to 350°F. Grease and flour a 10-inch tube or bundt pan.

Use an electric mixer to cream the butter and granulated sugar together until fluffy. Add the eggs one at a time, beating well after each addition. Sift together the flour, baking powder, and salt. Add the flour to the butter mixture in thirds, alternating each addition of flour with the addition of half the sour cream. Stir in the vanilla.

In a separate bowl, combine the brown sugar, cinnamon, and the pecans.

Pour one-third of the batter into the prepared pan. Sprinkle with half the streusel mixture. Pour another third of the batter into the pan and sprinkle with the remaining streusel mixture. Scrape the remaining batter into the pan and smooth the top. Bake for 1 hour, or until a toothpick inserted in the center comes out clean. Allow the cake to cool in the pan for 10 minutes. Remove the cake from the pan and cool on a wire rack.

When the cake is completely cooled, stir the glaze ingredients together in a small bowl until smooth. Drizzle over the cooled cake.

Kyle's Lemon Pound Cake

Serves 12

From Beth:
This cake is also good drizzled with Fresh Strawberry Sauce (page 180).

My nephew Kyle requests this cake every year on his birthday. You know that if this is a twelve-year-old boy's favorite cake, it's gotta be good!

3	cups all-purpose flour
½	teaspoon baking soda
½	teaspoon baking powder
¾	teaspoon salt
½	cup (1 stick) butter
½	cup vegetable shortening
2	cups sugar
4	large eggs
1	teaspoon vanilla extract
2	teaspoons freshly squeezed lemon juice
1	teaspoon finely grated lemon zest
1	cup buttermilk, well shaken

Preheat the oven to 350°F. Grease and flour a 10-inch tube pan.

Sift the flour together with the baking soda, baking powder, and salt. Set aside. In a large mixing bowl, beat the butter and shortening together until creamy, about 2 minutes. Add the sugar and beat an additional 5 minutes.

Add the eggs one at a time, beating only until the yolks disappear into the batter. Add the vanilla, lemon juice, and zest.

Add the flour mixture alternately with the buttermilk, beginning and ending with flour. Scrape the sides of the mixing bowl and beat only until well blended. Pour into the prepared pan and bake for 1 hour and 10 minutes. Cool slightly, then turn the cake out of the pan while it is still warm. Cool completely on a wire rack.

Just-Married Pound Cake

Serves 12

My wedding to Garth was such a wonderful day! We wanted it to be a small, private event, and it was, made possible by the help of our friends and families. Everybody was happy to pitch in and help—everybody except my mom, that is, when I asked her to make the wedding cake! I know, it sounds crazy, but I knew she could do it. My mom taught school for twenty-five years, but there was a period in her life (when she had me, to be exact) when she needed to be home. To earn extra money for the family, she began baking and selling cakes for birthday parties and weddings. She resumed her teaching career when I started first grade and retired in 1991 to run my fan club. (She has since retired from that too, and has gone back to being just Mom.)

She came out to Oklahoma the week before the wedding to make a wedding cake that I think turned out to be much bigger than she had been picturing, but it was simply stunning. She gave me the bride and groom decoration from her own wedding day, June 19, 1960, and it literally made the cake. My parents were very happily married for forty-five years, and the only thing that could have made my wedding day better would have been to have Daddy there. I think he was, though. He probably wouldn't have had any wedding cake, but he would have enjoyed the fried chicken and the barbecue!

My finished wedding cake took four electric mixers to make, but we've included the regular pound cake recipe here.

Gwen and Jack Yearwood at their wedding, June 19, 1960.

1½ cups (3 sticks) Blue Bonnet margarine, room temperature

1 1-pound box confectioners' sugar, box reserved

6 large eggs, room temperature

1 pound sifted cake flour

1 teaspoon vanilla extract

Preheat the oven to 300°F. Grease and flour a 9-inch tube pan.

Using a heavy-duty mixer, cream the margarine and sugar until the mixture is very light and fluffy, about 5 minutes.

One at a time, break the eggs into a small bowl, then add one at a time to the batter, beating only as long as it takes to break another egg into the small bowl between additions. Scrape down the sides of the mixing bowl.

From Gwen:
I can't believe I made this cake!

Measure the sifted flour into the empty confectioners' sugar box, filling it to the top. Add the flour to the sugar and egg mixture, stirring gently on low speed. Scrape the sides of the mixing bowl. Add the vanilla and mix again.

Pour the batter into the prepared pan and bake for 1 hour, or until the center is set. Check for doneness by touching the surface lightly with your fingertip or by inserting a toothpick in the center; it should come out clean.

Cool the cake in the pan for 10 minutes, then run a thin knife or spatula between the cake and the pan to loosen the edges and invert the cake onto a wire rack.

Garth's and my wedding cake from December 10, 2005.

White Cream Decorator Frosting

Using solid shortening instead of butter results in a pure white frosting that you can tint any color you like.

¾ cup solid white vegetable shortening, such as Crisco

1 pound confectioners' sugar

Pinch of salt

4–5 tablespoons very warm water

1½ teaspoons clear vanilla extract (see Note)

Note: If you can't find clear vanilla extract, you can use regular vanilla extract, but your icing won't be white. The regular extract will add a cream color to the icing.

Using an electric mixer, cream the shortening in a large bowl. Add the sugar gradually, blending well, and beat until fluffy. Beat in the salt, and then add the water by the tablespoon, beating continuously and adding just enough to achieve a smooth, spreadable consistency. Add the vanilla and beat on high until very fluffy. This frosting can be transferred to a pastry bag fitted with decorator tips for decorating cakes.

Buttercream Frosting

This recipe is basically the same as the White Cream Decorator Frosting except that, because you're not worried about the icing staying white, you can use milk and regular vanilla extract.

From Gwen: Add food colorings of your choice for decorating cakes and cookies.

¾ cup (1½ sticks) butter, room temperature

1 pound confectioners' sugar

4–5 tablespoons light cream or milk

1½ teaspoons vanilla extract

With an electric mixer, cream the butter and sugar together until smooth. Add the milk by the tablespoon, beating well after each addition and adding just enough liquid to make a smooth, spreadable icing. Add the vanilla and continue to beat the icing on high speed until it is very light and fluffy, about 5 minutes. Makes enough to frost the top and sides of 1 9-inch pound cake.

Chocolate Pound Cake

Serves 12

I like a good plain pound cake, but I also like it when I can find a way to make it a little bit different or special. Chocolate pound cake is so simple and so good. This cake is excellent served at room temperature or heated for 15 seconds in the microwave and topped with a scoop of vanilla ice cream.

- 3 cups all-purpose flour
- ½ teaspoon baking powder
- ½ teaspoon salt
- ½ cup cocoa
- 1 cup (2 sticks) butter, room temperature
- ½ cup vegetable shortening
- 3 cups sugar
- 5 large eggs, room temperature
- 1 cup milk
- 2 teaspoons vanilla extract

Preheat the oven to 350°F. Grease and flour a 10-inch tube pan.

Sift the flour, baking powder, salt, and cocoa together 3 times. Set aside.

With an electric mixer, cream the butter, shortening, and sugar until fluffy.

Add the eggs one at a time, beating well after each addition.

Add the flour mixture and the milk alternately, beginning and ending with flour. Add the vanilla.

Pour the batter into the prepared pan and bake for 1 hour. Check for doneness by inserting a toothpick into the cake. It should come out clean. Cool the cake in the pan for 30 minutes before turning it out onto a wire rack to cool completely.

German Chocolate Cake with Coconut Frosting

Serves 12

Every February, when Garth's birthday rolls around, I make this beautiful and delicious cake for him. Last fall, he made some sad statement like, "Only three more months until you make me that awesome German chocolate cake again!" I made the cake the next day. (I know, I'm a sucker.) I double the frosting recipe to frost the entire cake, because my husband likes extra frosting, but one recipe will frost the tops of the layers and do the trick just fine—unless you're Garth, of course!

If you have some left over, the frosting is also good spread on a graham cracker or on brownies (page 198). Okay, it's also good right off a spoon!

4	ounces sweet dark chocolate (see Shopping Hint, page 173)
1	cup (2 sticks) butter, at room temperature
¼	cup warm milk
2½	cups sifted cake flour
1	teaspoon baking soda
½	teaspoon salt
5	medium egg whites
2	cups sugar
5	medium egg yolks, at room temperature
1	teaspoon vanilla extract
¾	cup buttermilk, well shaken

From Gwen: Refrigerate the cake after it's frosted. Before serving, touch up any frosting that may have run down the sides.

continued . . .

Coconut Frosting

1 cup sugar

4 medium egg yolks

1 cup evaporated milk

½ cup (1 stick) butter

1 teaspoon vanilla extract

10 ounces fresh or frozen and thawed grated coconut

1½ cups finely ground pecans, walnuts, or almonds

Prepare the chocolate by melting it in the top of a double boiler, stirring until it is smooth. Add ¼ cup (½ stick) of the butter and stir until it is melted and blended. Add ¼ cup of warm milk and stir until smooth. Set the chocolate aside to cool.

Preheat the oven to 350°F.

Line the bottoms only of 3 9-inch cake pans with circles of parchment paper, or grease each pan bottom only with solid shortening and dust lightly with flour. Sift together the sifted and measured flour, baking soda, and salt.

Whip the egg whites until stiff using the wire beater of the mixer. Transfer the beaten whites to a separate bowl and set aside.

In the mixer bowl, cream the remaining 1½ sticks of butter and sugar together until fluffy. Add the egg yolks one at a time, beating well after each addition (see "From Trisha," opposite). Add the melted, cooled chocolate and the vanilla. Mix well.

With the mixer on very low, stir in the flour mixture alternately with the buttermilk. Do this by adding about a third of the flour and slowly stirring it in completely. Then add about half the buttermilk and stir it in. Continue adding flour and buttermilk in this manner, ending with flour. Scrape the sides and bottom of the bowl and stir again. With a long-handled spoon or spatula, fold and stir the beaten egg whites into the batter until the batter is smooth with no visible clumps of whites.

Divide the batter evenly between the prepared pans and bake for 30 to 40 minutes. Bake on the middle rack of the oven, allowing at least ¼-inch clearance between the pans and the oven walls. The cake will rise above the pan edges as it bakes but will not spill over and will settle back down as it continues to bake. The cake is done when it begins to pull away from the sides of the pans and springs back to a light touch. Cool layers in the pans for about 8 minutes.

Run a knife around the edges of each pan and turn the layers out onto wire racks that have been sprayed with cooking spray. Cool layers completely before frosting.

To make the frosting, combine the sugar, egg yolks, and evaporated milk in the top of a double boiler. Stir with a wire whisk until the yolks are fully incorporated. Add the butter. Place over simmering water and bring to a boil (see Note). Simmer for 12 to 15 minutes longer, stirring constantly, until the mixture thickens. Add the vanilla, coconut, and nuts. Cool.

To assemble the cake, place one layer on a cake stand and spread with frosting. Frost each layer completely, top and sides, as it is added to the cake.

From Trisha: Separated egg yolks will slide easily and individually from a small bowl if the bowl is rinsed with water first.

Note: You can also make the frosting in a regular saucepan, but be sure to stir it constantly, as it scorches quite easily. Also, you *must* use the finely grated fresh or frozen coconut, not canned or shredded, to be able to spread the frosting on the sides of the cake easily.

Shopping Hint: For those cooks who use a lot of sweet baking chocolate, the chocolate used in this recipe can be purchased in bulk online at www.cocoasupply.com. Choose La Equatoriale—Dark Chocolate Coverture. The cost, including postage, is half what you would probably pay in grocery stores. Share the large bar with your friends who bake.

Lizzie's Old-Fashioned Cocoa Cake with Caramel Icing

So what's my birthday cake of choice? Chocolate cake with caramel icing. Yum! Most people have tried white cake with caramel icing, but my grandma Elizabeth Yearwood spread that amazing Caramel Icing on chocolate layers, and it was even more delicious. The cake recipe came from my grandma Paulk. I guess I could call this Two-Grandma Cake! Now my mom makes this cake for me every year. The Caramel Icing has a mind of its own, so you never really know what it's going to look like, but it doesn't matter to me. It always tastes amazing!

- 2 cups all-purpose flour
- ⅔ cup cocoa
- 1¼ teaspoons baking soda
- ¼ teaspoon baking powder
- 1 teaspoon salt
- ⅔ cup (1⅓ sticks) butter
- 1⅔ cups sugar
- 3 large eggs
- ½ teaspoon vanilla extract
- 1⅓ cups water

Caramel Icing

- 4 cups sugar
- 1 cup milk
- 1 stick (½ cup) butter
- ⅛ teaspoon baking soda
- 1 teaspoon vanilla

Preheat the oven to 350°F. Grease and lightly flour 2 9-inch cake pans.

Sift together the flour, cocoa, baking soda and powder, and salt, and set aside. With an electric mixer, cream the butter and sugar until fluffy, about 5 minutes. Add the eggs and vanilla and beat on high speed for 3 minutes. Add the flour mixture alternately with 1⅓ cups water, beginning and ending with flour.

Divide the batter evenly between the pans and bake for 30 to 35 minutes. Turn the layers out onto racks that have been sprayed with cooking spray.

Mix 3 cups of the sugar and the milk in a heavy 3-quart saucepan. Bring slowly to a boil and keep it hot. Caramelize remaining cup of sugar in an iron skillet. Do this by cooking over medium-high heat and stirring and scraping the pan with a flat-edged spatula as the sugar melts. Continue to cook until the syrup turns to medium or dark brown in color. This occurs at about 320°F to 350°F on a candy thermometer. Do not scorch the syrup. Stream the syrup into the boiling sugar and milk mixture and cook to the soft ball stage, about 238°F. Add the butter, soda, and vanilla.

Pour the hot mixture into the metal bowl of an electric mixer and beat as it cools until the icing is creamy, 15 to 20 minutes. Spread on the cake layers while the icing is still warm. If it becomes too stiff, add a few drops of hot water.

Note: Makes more than enough to frost 2 9-inch cake layers. Leftover frosting can be stored in the refrigerator for up to 2 weeks, rewarmed, and used to frost brownies or cupcakes.

Beth and me with Beth's piano birthday cake made by Gwen.

Pineapple Upside-Down Cake

Serves 4

From Gwen: So moist!

I'm always looking for fun recipes to make with our girls, hoping they will grow up to love cooking as much as I do. This cake is fun because they can't believe you put all the pretty decorations on the bottom of the pan and the cake still turns out to be gorgeous!

3	tablespoons butter
½	cup light brown sugar, packed
9	canned pineapple slices in juice, drained
5	maraschino cherries
1½	cups sifted all-purpose flour
2	teaspoons baking powder
¼	teaspoon salt
⅓	cup solid vegetable shortening
⅔	cup granulated sugar
1	large egg
¾	teaspoon vanilla extract
⅔	cup milk

Preheat the oven to 350°F.

Place the butter in an 8 x 8 x 2-inch square pan and put it in the oven to melt. When the butter is melted, carefully remove the pan from the oven and sprinkle the brown sugar over the butter. Arrange the pineapple rings on top of the sugar in a single layer, making 3 rows. Cut the maraschino cherries in half and place 1 half in the center of each pineapple ring, cut side up. Set the pan aside.

Sift the flour, baking powder, and salt, then sift once more. Set aside.

Using an electric mixer, cream the shortening and the granulated sugar together until light and fluffy. Add the egg and beat until fully combined. Add the vanilla. Blend in the flour mixture alternately with the milk, beginning and ending with flour. Stir only enough after each addition to combine.

Pour the batter carefully into the pineapple-lined pan. Bake for 40 minutes and test for doneness by inserting a toothpick in the center or pressing the cake lightly with a fingertip; if the impression springs back, the cake is done. Run a knife around the edges of the pan and place a serving dish on top. Invert the cake onto the serving plate. Leave the pan inverted over the cake for several minutes to allow the syrup to soak into the cake.

From Trisha: You may have to cut the pineapple rings a little bit to make them smaller, so all nine fit in the pan.

Iced Italian Cream Cake

Serves 12

We seem to place a lot of emphasis on birthday cakes in my family. We like for everyone to have his or her favorite cake, but more than that, we like the variety of awesome sweets we get to eat throughout the year! This cake was once Beth's birthday cake of choice—or so Mom thought until she learned that Beth actually preferred the chocolate caramel cake I always ask for. At first, I thought she was just trying to copy me (it's a sister thing!), but then I realized that if it's her favorite cake, too, that's twice a year for me!

This is great tasting, very pretty, and very easy. It deserves to be a first choice, too.

- 2 cups all-purpose flour
- 1 teaspoon baking soda
- ½ cup (1 stick) unsalted butter
- ½ cup vegetable shortening
- 2 cups sugar
- 5 large eggs, separated
- 1 cup buttermilk, well shaken
- 1 teaspoon vanilla extract
- ½ cup chopped pecans
- 1 cup sweetened shredded coconut

Italian Cream Frosting

- 8 ounces cream cheese, room temperature
- 4 tablespoons (½ stick) butter, room temperature
- 1 pound confectioners' sugar
- 1 teaspoon vanilla extract
- ½ cup chopped nuts

Preheat the oven to 350°F. Grease and lightly flour 3 9-inch cake pans.

Sift the flour and soda together and set aside.

With an electric mixer, cream the butter and shortening with the sugar until fluffy, about 5 minutes. Add the egg yolks one at a time, beating well between each addition. With the mixer on medium speed, add the flour and buttermilk alternately, beginning and ending with buttermilk. Add the vanilla, coconut, and nuts, and stir well to incorporate.

In a separate bowl with clean beaters, whip the egg whites to stiff peaks. Gently fold the beaten egg whites into the batter, just until blended.

Pour the batter into the prepared pans and bake for 25 minutes. Test for doneness by touching the top of the cake with your finger. The cake is done if it bounces back up. Cool the layers on wire racks sprayed with cooking spray to prevent sticking.

With an electric mixer, beat the cream cheese with the butter on the high speed until fluffy. Reduce the speed to medium and blend in the sugar and vanilla. Beat well until the frosting is smooth.

When the cake is completely cool, spread the frosting between the layers and on the sides and top of the cake. Sprinkle with the nuts.

Trisha and Beth with Lizzie's chocolate cake with caramel icing and iced Italian cream cake for their birthdays in September 1982.

Cakes, Pies, and Puddings   179

Joe's "Say Cheese" Cheesecake with Fresh Strawberry Sauce

Serves 8 to 10

It has become a tradition in my house that I make everyone's favorite dessert on his or her birthday. Garth's favorite is German Chocolate Cake, Taylor's is Banana Pudding, and so on. When it came time for my friend Joe's birthday, his wife, Kim, let me know that *his* favorite was cheesecake. "No problem," I said, as I started thinking about that awesome cheesecake in a box I was going to make (I have to admit that it's my favorite). "He loves the old-style New York cheesecake," she explained. Umm . . . no problem? But I was committed, so I did what I always do: call my family for help. Beth hooked me up with several cheesecake recipes, and this is the one I like best. It made me a big hit on Joe's birthday.

From Beth: The strawberry sauce is good served on pound cake or angel food cake, too.

Note: The water bath prevents the cheesecake from cracking as it bakes.

Crust
1½ cups fine graham cracker crumbs

¼ cup sugar

¼ cup (½ stick) butter, melted

Filling
32 ounces (4 8-ounce packages) cream cheese

2 cups sour cream

4 large eggs

1¼ cups sugar

2½ tablespoons cornstarch

2 teaspoons vanilla extract

Fresh Strawberry Sauce
1¼ cups fresh strawberries

¼ cup sugar

1½ teaspoons grated lime zest

Preheat the oven to 375°F. Spray the bottom of 10-inch springform pan with cooking spray, line the bottom with a round of parchment paper, and spray the paper with cooking spray. Place the pan on a sheet of heavy-duty aluminum foil and bring the foil up to enclose the seam between the bottom and sides.

To make the crust, stir together the graham cracker crumbs, sugar, and butter in a mixing bowl until the crumbs are coated. Press the mixture firmly into the bottom of the pan and up the sides. Set aside.

In a large bowl, beat the cream cheese with the sour cream. Add the eggs, one at a time, beating well after each addition. Add the sugar, corn-starch, and vanilla, and beat until smooth.

Pour the batter into the prepared crust. Place the foil-wrapped pan in a larger pan placed on the oven rack. Carefully pour ½-inch warm water into the larger pan (see Note). Bake for 1 hour. Turn off the oven and open the door. Let the cheesecake stand in the opened oven for 1 hour. Refrigerate the cheesecake for 2 hours or overnight before removing from the pan.

To make the sauce, process all ingredients in a food processor or blender until they are smooth. Chill for at least 1 hour. (This sauce is best if served cold from the refrigerator.)

Basic Pastry

Makes 2
9-inch pie crusts

There are some really good ready-to-use piecrusts on the market these days. My favorite is Mrs. Smith's deep-dish frozen pie shells. Still, if you have time, it's always better to make your own! This pie shell can be used for recipes that call for baked or unbaked crusts.

- 2 cups sifted all-purpose flour
- 1 teaspoon salt
- ⅔ cup chilled solid shortening

  About 6 tablespoons ice water

Sift the flour and the salt together into a cold medium bowl. Cut in ⅓ cup of the shortening with two knives or a pastry blender until the mixture resembles cornmeal. Cut in the remaining ⅓ cup shortening until the mixture gathers into small pea-sized pieces. Sprinkle the ice water, 1 tablespoon at a time, over a small portion of the mixture. Use a fork to press the mixture together, making a small ball of dough. Sprinkle another tablespoon of water over another dry portion of the flour and press it together. Continue moistening small portions of the dry mixture until all of the flour is moistened. Use only enough water to make the dough stick together. It should not be wet or slippery. Press all the moistened portions together gently and quickly with your fingers. Do not knead. The less the dough is handled, the more tender and flaky the pastry will be. Cover and chill the dough.

On a lightly floured board or canvas, roll out half of the dough into a circle ⅛ inch thick and about 2 inches larger than the pie pan. Fold the circle in half to fit it loosely into the pie pan. Trim the excess dough with scissors, leaving about 1 inch of the pastry over the edge of the pan to be folded under to form a standing, fluted rim.

For a prebaked crust, press foil gently into the pan over the pastry and prick the bottom with the times of a fork to prevent air bubbles from forming during baking. Fill with pie weights or dried beans. Bake at 350°F for 15 to 20 minutes, or until lighter golden.

Sweet Potato Pie

Sweet Potato Pie is always served at Thanksgiving at my house. I used to think there wasn't much of a difference between Sweet Potato Pie and Pumpkin Pie, but this recipe made me change my mind. It's just sweet enough, and it's so smooth and creamy. Hmmm . . . I need to think of more holidays to make this for, so I can eat it more often!

1½ cups pureéd sweet potatoes, canned or home-baked (page 147)

1 cup sugar

2 large eggs

¼ cup (½ stick) butter, softened

¼ cup milk

¼ teaspoon ground cinnamon

¼ teaspoon ground nutmeg

Pinch of salt

1 teaspoon vanilla extract

2 unbaked 9-inch pie shells, homemade (page 182) or purchased

Preheat the oven to 300°F.

In the bowl of an electric mixer, combine the potatoes, ½ cup sugar, and the eggs, butter, milk, cinnamon, nutmeg, salt, and vanilla. Beat until thoroughly blended and smooth. Divide evenly between the pie shells. Sprinkle ¼ cup sugar over each pie. Allow the pies to stand for 15 minutes before baking to allow the sugar to melt. Bake the pies for 1 hour, or until a toothpick inserted in the center comes out clean. Cool them before serving.

Makes 2 9-inch pies; serves 16 to 20

From Gwen: A sweet potato never tasted so good! The added sugar on top gives just the right finishing crunch.

Pecan Pie

Serves 8

Every Georgia girl has a trusted pecan pie recipe if she knows what's good for her! This one came from a great family friend in Monticello named Betty Maxwell.

- 1 cup light brown sugar, packed
- ½ cup granulated sugar
- 2 large eggs
- ½ cup (1 stick) butter, melted
- 1½ teaspoons vanilla extract
- 2 tablespoons milk
- 1 tablespoon all-purpose flour
- 1 cup chopped pecans
- 1 9-inch deep-dish pie shell, unbaked, or homemade pastry (page 182)
- 1 cup pecan halves

Preheat the oven to 325°F.

To make the filling, beat the sugars with the eggs in an electric mixer until creamy, about 5 minutes. Add the melted butter, vanilla, milk, flour, and chopped pecans. Pour the mixture into the shell. Arrange the pecan halves on top of the pie in a circular pattern.

Bake the pie for 55 minutes. Check for doneness by shaking the pan slightly. The pie should be firm, with only a slight jiggle in the center. It will set more as it cools. Serve warm, topped with vanilla ice cream, or at room temperature with a dollop of whipped cream.

French Coconut Pie

From Gwen:
The coconut rises
to the top to form
a crunchy
topping.

You can make the homemade pastry recipe if you like, but if you start with a purchased pie crust, this is a really quick and easy dessert. Be sure to use grated fresh or frozen coconut for ease in slicing.

1½ cups sugar

1 tablespoon all-purpose flour

½ cup (1 stick) butter, melted

3 large eggs

½ cup buttermilk, well shaken

1 teaspoon vanilla extract

2 cups grated coconut, fresh or frozen

1 deep-dish unbaked 9-inch pie shell, homemade (page 182) or purchased

Preheat the oven to 350°F.

In the bowl of an electric mixer, beat the sugar and flour with the melted butter. Add the eggs one at a time, mixing well after each. Add the buttermilk and vanilla and combine again. Stir in the coconut.

Pour the filling into the prepared pie shell. Bake for 45 to 50 minutes, or until lightly brown and the center of the pie doesn't jiggle when shaken lightly. A toothpick inserted into the center of the pie should come out moist but not covered with custard. The coconut will rise to form a top crust during baking. Set the pie in the pan on a wire rack and cool completely before serving.

Butterscotch Pie

When my brother-in-law John turned fifty, my sister, Beth, wanted to make a really special dessert for him. She remembered his mentioning a favorite butterscotch pie his mother, Blanche, used to make and this recipe came from her. It was a big hit on his birthday.

- 1 cup light brown sugar, packed
- 3 tablespoons butter
- 4 tablespoons heavy cream
- 2 cups milk
- 3 tablespoons cornstarch
- 3 large eggs, separated
- ½ teaspoon vanilla extract
- Pinch of salt
- ¼ cup granulated sugar
- 1 9-inch pie crust, homemade (page 182) or purchased, prebaked as directed

Preheat the oven to 350°F.

In a medium saucepan, stir together the brown sugar, butter, and cream. Cook over medium heat until the sugar dissolves and the mixture comes to a full boil, becoming thick and brown, about 5 minutes.

In a measuring cup, mix the milk, cornstarch, egg yolks, and vanilla together. Add to the sugar mixture, stirring constantly, and cook until thick, about 3 minutes. Pour the filling into the prebaked pie crust.

Make the meringue by beating the egg whites with a pinch of salt until they begin to get stiff. Add the granulated sugar and continue beating until the whites are stiff and hold peaks. Spread the meringue on top of the pie, taking care to spread it to the edges of the crust. Bake until light brown.

Blackberry Cobbler

Serves 10

After moving to Oklahoma in 2002, I discovered an abundance of wild blackberries growing on our farm. Channeling my best Martha Stewart, I decided I *had* to pick these berries myself and prepare the perfect blackberry cobbler for my family. (This is also where I learned about the abundance of chiggers in Oklahoma, something we call red bugs in Georgia. They apparently love to feast on unsuspecting berry pickers.) After talking a couple of my girlfriends into going blackberry picking with me, I had an ample supply of beautiful blackberries. When I called my mom, the goddess of all things culinary, to ask for Grandma Paulk's blackberry cobbler recipe, I got the familiar reply: "Well, actually there is no real recipe." Ahhh! My notes from that day go something like this:

Berries in water
Sugar
Bring to a boil
Flour
Shortening
Milk

From Trisha: The last time I made this, I didn't have time to make homemade pastry, so I tried store-bought refrigerated roll-out pastry shells and cut them into strips. It worked great!

You get the picture. The cobbler actually came out great, and I was proud of my handpicked berries, but truth be told, it was the first and last time I picked the berries wild. Store-bought berries at your local grocery or farmer's market are usually plumper and sweeter than wild berries. If you use wild berries, you will probably need to add more sugar.

continued . . .

¾ cup sugar

2 cups plus 1 tablespoon self-rising flour (see Note)

2 cups fresh blackberries

¼ cup (½ stick) butter, cold, cut into small pieces

½–⅔ cup milk

Vanilla ice cream for serving

Preheat the oven to 450°F. Butter a 1-quart casserole dish or baking pan.

In a medium saucepan combine the sugar, 1 tablespoon of the flour, berries, and 1 cup water. Bring to a boil, reduce the heat, and simmer for 2 minutes, then remove from the heat and set aside.

In a medium bowl, use a pastry blender or two knives to cut the butter into the remaining 2 cups flour. Stir in just enough milk to make a soft dough that pulls away from the sides of the bowl. Turn the dough out on a lightly floured board and pat into a square. Use a rolling pin to roll it to ½ inch thick. Cut the dough into 2-inch-wide strips.

Pour 1 cup of the blackberry mixture into the bottom of the pan. Arrange half of the dough strips on top of the blackberry mix, placing them close together. Bake until brown, about 12 minutes, then remove from the oven and pour the remaining berry mixture over the baked strips. Arrange another layer of dough strips on top and bake for 12 more minutes, or until brown. Serve warm with ice cream.

Note: If you don't have self-rising flour, substitute 2 cups all-purpose flour mixed with 3 teaspoons baking powder and ¼ teaspoon salt.

Easy Peach Cobbler

Serves 8

From Trisha: This forms its own top crust while it bakes.

Note: If you don't have self-rising flour, substitute 1 cup all-purpose flour mixed with 1½ teaspoons baking powder and ⅛ teaspoon salt.

You can't be considered a serious southern cook if you don't know how to make peach cobbler. Canned or frozen fruit works better in some recipes than fresh, and this is a perfect example. I recommend any brand of canned freestone peaches because they are tender and tasty. This dessert is easy to make and it tastes delicious, especially with a huge dollop of Home-Churned Ice Cream (page 212) on top.

2   15-ounce cans sliced peaches in syrup
½   cup (1 stick) butter
1   cup self-rising flour (see Note)
1   cup sugar
1   cup milk

Preheat the oven to 350°F. Drain 1 can of peaches; reserve the syrup from the other.

Place the butter in a 9 x 12-inch ovenproof baking dish. Heat the butter in the oven until it's melted. In a medium bowl, mix the flour and sugar. Stir in the milk and the reserved syrup. Carefully remove the baking dish from the oven and pour the batter over the melted butter. Arrange the peaches over the batter. Bake for 1 hour. The cobbler is done when the batter rises around the peaches and the crust is thick and golden brown. Serve warm with vanilla ice cream.

From Gwen:
Two types of peaches, freestone and clingstone, are just what the terms suggest. The flesh of a ripe freestone variety pulls easily away from the pit or stone, while the clingstone flesh, well, clings! Go online to www.lanepacking.com for all the scoop on Georgia peaches.

Bret's Banana Pudding, Aunt T Style

My nephew Bret is allergic to eggs, which always presents a challenge when it comes to dessert. The bigger challenge is that Bret loves banana pudding. When a seven-year-old boy who is very cute asks why everyone else is having banana pudding while he is not, Aunt Trisha has to think quickly, and because my regular recipe calls for four eggs, I have to get really creative. This banana pudding recipe came about on the spot, and Bret isn't the only one who loves it!

Serves 1 hungry nephew

6   vanilla wafers

1   medium banana, sliced

½   cup nondairy topping, such as Cool Whip

On a dessert plate, make a layer of vanilla wafers and sliced bananas. Top with Cool Whip and serve!

Bret eating "his" banana pudding.

Banana Pudding

Serves 8

From Gwen:
Wait, if you can, to allow the wafers to become soft before serving.

We should rename this recipe Goldilocks Pudding! My mother's notes say she made several attempts at my dad's favorite dessert before coming up with this particular version—not too hard, not too soft. It has become a mainstay in my home, too. Garth prefers the pudding without the meringue, so I usually make two versions, one with and one without. Either way, it's a homey, satisfying finish to any meal.

4	large eggs
¾	cup sugar
3	tablespoons all-purpose flour
½	teaspoon salt
2	cups milk
½	teaspoon vanilla extract
30–40	vanilla wafers
5–6	medium ripe bananas
	Pinch of salt

Separate the yolks from the whites of 3 eggs. Set aside the whites. In the top of a double boiler, whisk together ½ cup of the sugar, the flour, and the salt. Stir in the whole egg and the 3 yolks, and then stir in the milk.

Cook uncovered, stirring often, for about 10 minutes, or until the mixture thickens. Remove from the heat and stir in the vanilla.

Preheat the oven to 425°F.

Spread a thin layer of pudding in a 1½-quart casserole dish. Arrange a layer of vanilla wafers on top of the pudding. Thinly slice the bananas crosswise, about ⅛ inch thick, and arrange a layer of banana slices over the wafers. Spread one-third of the remaining pudding over the bananas and continue layering wafers, bananas, and pudding, ending with pudding.

To make the meringue, beat the reserved egg whites with a pinch of salt until they are stiff. Gradually beat in the remaining ¼ cup sugar and continue beating until the whites will not slide out of the mixing bowl when it is tilted. Spread the meringue over the pudding with a spatula, making a few decorative peaks on top, and bake for 5 minutes, or until the meringue is lightly browned.

cookies, candy, and ice cream

I've always claimed that I'm not much of a sweets person, that I prefer salty dishes, but I guess it would be more accurate to say I am not a big fan of store-bought sweets. If I'm going to eat something sweet, I would rather hold out for homemade brownies or cookies than waste my calories on something out of a box. And with the invention of electric ice-cream churns, making homemade ice cream has become a piece of cake! (Did I really just say that?)

I love to give homemade baked goods as gifts at Christmas. It says you think enough of the recipient to make something with your own two hands just for them. Cookies, candy, and fudge are relatively easy, inexpensive ways to give that gift. Of course, once the smell of baking chocolate chip cookies starts to waft through my house, I have a hard time giving anything away. Sometimes you need to give that gift to yourself, too!

Most of these recipes say to store leftovers in an airtight container for up to two weeks. Keep in mind that this was an educated guess. I would personally like to meet someone who has leftover cookies in their home for two weeks! My crowd can make a dozen cookies disappear in a matter of seconds.

Brownies

From Gwen:
I always double
this recipe and
bake it in a
9 x 13 x 2-inch
pan.

I love these brownies plain, but Garth likes them frosted, so I usually make some Coconut Frosting (page 172) on the side just for him. The unsweetened baking chocolate keeps the brownies from being too sweet. I know, sweets are supposed to be sweet, but trust me, these are just right!

2 ounces unsweetened baking chocolate

⅓ cup solid vegetable shortening, such as Crisco

2 large eggs

1 cup sugar

⅔ cup all-purpose flour

½ teaspoon baking powder

½ teaspoon salt

1 cup chopped pecans

1 teaspoon vanilla extract

Preheat the oven to 350°F. Grease the bottom of an 8 x 8 x 2-inch pan.

Melt the chocolate and shortening together over simmering water or in the microwave. Cool slightly. In a mixing bowl, beat the eggs well. Add the sugar and combine thoroughly, then stir in the chocolate mixture.

Sift the flour together with the baking powder and salt, then stir into the chocolate mixture. Stir in the nuts and vanilla.

Spread the batter evenly in the prepared pan. Bake for 25 to 30 minutes, or until a toothpick inserted in the center comes out clean. Cool in the pan for 5 minutes, then cut into 2-inch squares. These are good warm or cold.

Chewy Chocolate Chip Cookies

I started making these cookies in the eighth grade, and they just might be responsible for my love of cooking. It wasn't just that they are gooey and awesome, which they are; it was also that people complimented me on my cooking skills, and that gave me confidence. It later worked out in the singing thing, too! Exactly how chewy these cookies are depends on how big you make them. I make mine a little bigger than the recipe calls for because I like them soft in the middle. They are best served with a really cold glass of milk . . . or more cookies!

⅔ cup (1⅓ sticks) butter, room temperature

¾ cup granulated sugar

¼ cup dark brown sugar, packed

1 large egg, room temperature

1 teaspoon vanilla extract

1¾ cups sifted all-purpose flour

½ teaspoon baking soda

½ teaspoon salt

1 cup (1 6-ounce package) semisweet chocolate chips

Place the oven rack in the center of the oven and preheat the oven to 375°F.

Using the electric mixer, beat the butter, sugars, egg, and vanilla together until smooth.

Sift the flour, baking soda, and salt together and, with the beater running, slowly add to the butter mixture. Stir in the chocolate chips.

Drop the batter by teaspoonfuls about 2 inches apart on an ungreased cookie sheet. Bake for 8 to 10 minutes, or until lightly browned. Carefully remove the cookies to a wire rack to cool. Store in an air-tight container.

Snickerdoodles

Makes 4 to
5 dozen

One of our girls doesn't like chocolate! Hard to believe if you're a chocolate lover like me, but I'm always looking for a chocolate alternative for dessert around my house. Fortunately, this was Beth's specialty growing up, and I've stolen her recipe for my own.

½ cup salted butter

½ cup vegetable shortening

1½ cups plus 2 tablespoons sugar

2 medium eggs

2¾ cups all-purpose flour

2 teaspoons cream of tartar

1 teaspoon baking soda

¼ teaspoon salt

2 teaspoons ground cinnamon

Preheat the oven to 400°F. In a large bowl, combine the butter, shortening, 1½ cups sugar, and the eggs and mix thoroughly. Sift together the flour, cream of tartar, baking soda, and salt, and stir into the shortening mixture.

In a small bowl, stir together the remaining 2 tablespoons sugar with the cinnamon. Shape the dough into 1½-inch balls and roll each ball in the cinnamon sugar. Arrange the dough balls 2 inches apart on an ungreased cookie sheet. Bake 8 to 10 minutes. Transfer the cookies to wire racks for cooling. Store in an airtight container.

Cinnamon Cookies

The original recipe for these cinnamon cookies is written on an index card in my sister Beth's earliest cursive handwriting, and it is probably the first recipe I remember her making when we were girls. She still makes them every Halloween.

Makes 2 dozen

2 cups all-purpose flour

1 teaspoon baking soda

½ teaspoon salt

1 teaspoon ground cinnamon

1 teaspoon ground cloves

1 teaspoon ground ginger

¾ cup solid vegetable shortening, such as Crisco

1½ cups sugar

¼ cup molasses

1 large egg

Preheat the oven to 350°F.

Onto a large piece of waxed paper, sift together the flour, baking soda, salt, cinnamon, cloves, and ginger. In a large mixing bowl, cream the shortening and 1 cup of the sugar. Add the flour mixture to the sugar mixture and combine. Mix in the molasses and the egg. Cover the dough in plastic wrap and chill for 1 hour, or until firm. Roll the dough into 1-inch balls, and then roll balls in the remaining sugar before placing on an ungreased cookie sheet, 1 to 1½ inches apart. Bake for 20 minutes. Transfer the cookies to a wire rack to cool. Store in an airtight container.

Gingerbread Cookies

Makes 5 dozen

Note: Keep the bowl and the decorator tips covered with a moist cloth to prevent the icing from hardening prematurely.

I have always liked the smell of gingerbread cookies baking. It reminds me of my favorite holiday, Christmas, but I bake these cookies year round. My sister is the gingerbread house queen. I have made just one gingerbread house in my life—I'm not really patient enough to do the job justice!

1 cup vegetable shortening

1 cup sugar

1 large egg

1 cup molasses

2 tablespoons cider vinegar

4–5 cups sifted all-purpose flour

1½ teaspoons baking soda

½ teaspoon salt

3 teaspoons ground ginger

1 teaspoon ground cinnamon

1 teaspoon ground cloves

Using an electric mixer, cream the shortening and sugar together until light and fluffy. Add the egg, molasses, and vinegar and beat on high speed to blend thoroughly. Sift together 4 cups of the flour and the baking soda, salt, ginger, cinnamon, and cloves. Add the dry ingredients to the creamed shortening and sugar and mix to make a firm, manageable dough, adding more flour if needed. Wrap the dough in plastic and refrigerate for 3 hours or until firm.

Preheat the oven to 375°F. Lightly grease 1 or 2 baking sheets.

Spray a rolling pin with cooking spray and lightly flour your work surface. Roll the dough to ⅛-inch thickness and cut it into desired shapes with a knife or cookie cutters. (You can reroll the scraps to make a few more cookies.) Place the cookies 1 inch apart on the prepared baking sheet and bake for 5 to 6 minutes.

Cool the cookies for 2 minutes on the cookie sheet before removing to a wire rack to cool completely.

Royal Icing

3   egg whites, room temperature, or equivalent meringue powder

2½   cups sifted confectioners' sugar

¼   teaspoon cream of tartar

Beat the egg whites and ⅓ cup of the sugar with a wire whisk or the whisk attachment on your mixer. Add another ⅓ cup sugar and the cream of tartar and beat 10 minutes longer. Add the remaining sugar and beat until the mixture is smooth and thick. The icing can be tinted as desired with food coloring.

Note: To make gingerbread house sections, spray the back of a jelly roll pan and a rolling pin with cooking spray. Roll out the dough to ⅛-inch thickness and place on the back of the jelly roll pan. Cut out the desired shapes for the walls and roof, then remove the trimmings (you can save and reroll these scraps for cookies or additional house embellishments) and bake for 5 to 6 minutes. Cool for 2 minutes on the pan before carefully removing to a cooling rack. Cool completely before assembling the gingerbread house. Use Royal Icing (see recipe above) to glue the gingerbread house together and to decorate the cookies.

Trisha's gingerbread house from 1982.

Bret Bernard eating a gingerbread house.

Crescent Cookies

Makes 2 dozen

From Gwen:
You may know these as Wedding Cookies or Melting Moments.

The tradition of making homemade treats for gifts is still alive and well in the South. In the early to mid-1990s, I worked on videos and photo shoots in Nashville with a girl named Maria Smoot. She is responsible for some of the most beautiful hairstyles in country music. I found a tin of these cookies in my mailbox one Christmas with a sweet note from Maria. What was even sweeter was that she included the recipe.

- 1   cup (2 sticks) salted butter, room temperature
- 1   cup confectioners' sugar
- 1/8   teaspoon salt
- 2   teaspoons vanilla extract
- 2¼   cups sifted all-purpose flour
- ½   cup finely chopped pecans

Preheat the oven to 325°F.

In the bowl of an electric mixer, cream together the butter, ¼ cup of the sugar, the salt, and the vanilla until light and fluffy. Beat in the flour, and then stir in the pecans by hand.

Shape the dough into 1-inch balls. Roll each ball slightly and form into a half-moon crescent. Arrange the shaped cookies 2 inches apart on lightly greased cookie sheets. Bake for 15 minutes, or until the edges are slightly browned but the tops are still pale. Transfer the cookies to a rack to cool.

Put the remaining ¾ cup sugar in a shallow bowl. Roll the cooled cookies in the sugar, coating liberally. Store in an airtight container.

Mari's Oatmeal Cookies

Makes 4 dozen

From Beth:
It's the coconut in these cookies that makes them really good!

Beth's friend Mari sent these cookies with her on a family trip to Rosemary Beach, Florida, several summers ago. It was the first time my entire family had vacationed with Garth and the girls. I think these cookies started to quickly disappear shortly after Garth arrived!

1 cup (2 sticks) salted butter, room temperature

1 cup brown sugar, packed

1 cup granulated sugar

2 large eggs

1 teaspoon vanilla extract

2 cups sifted all-purpose flour

1 teaspoon baking soda

1 teaspoon baking powder

¼ teaspoon salt

2 cups old-fashioned oatmeal, such as Quaker

1 cup chopped pecans

1 cup grated coconut

Preheat the oven to 375°F.

In an electric mixer, cream the butter and the sugars. Add the eggs and vanilla and beat well. Sift together the flour, baking soda, baking powder, and salt, and add to the butter mixture. Add the oatmeal, nuts, and coconut.

Drop the dough by teaspoonfuls onto an ungreased baking sheet 2 inches apart. Bake for 10 minutes, or until light brown. Cool on the baking sheet for 2 minutes before transferring to a wire rack to cool completely. The cookies will be chewy.

Skillet Almond Shortbread

Who ever heard of baking a dessert in a cast-iron skillet? You have now! The heavy pan ensures that the shortbread cooks evenly to a beautiful pale color top and bottom.

1¾ cups sugar

¾ cup (1½ sticks) butter, melted

2 large eggs

1½ cups all-purpose flour

½ teaspoon salt

1 teaspoon almond extract

½ cup sliced almonds with skins

Preheat the oven to 350°F. Line a 10-inch cast-iron skillet with aluminum foil and spray the foil with cooking spray. Alternatively, place a circle of parchment paper in the bottom of the skillet, then lightly grease or oil the paper.

In a large mixing bowl, stir 1½ cups of the sugar into the melted butter. Beat in the eggs one at a time. Sift the flour and salt onto the batter. Add the flavoring and stir well. Pour the batter into the skillet. Top with the sliced almonds and the remaining ¼ cup sugar. Bake for 35 minutes, or until slightly brown on top. Cool the shortbread in the skillet. When cool, use the foil to lift the shortbread from the skillet; remove the foil before serving. If you have used the parchment liner instead, run a sharp knife around the sides of the shortbread and invert the pan to remove it; peel off the parchment paper.

Serves 10

From Beth:
My friend Phyllis brought this to our girls-only beach trip last year. It became an instant hit. It's a great leftover . . . if there's any left over!

Nutty Orange Biscotti

From Trisha:
I usually leave the fancy recipes to my sister, and this is one of hers, but it's easy to make. They look so fancy on the plate, and sound so cool, though, that people will think you worked really hard to make them.

Don't be surprised at how sticky this dough is as you're trying to shape it into a log for the first baking! After it comes out of the oven, it's easy to cut into biscotti slices. Cooking the slices slowly on both sides gives it that nice biscotti crunch.

4	large eggs
1	cup sugar
1½	tablespoons grated orange zest
2	tablespoons vegetable oil
½	teaspoon vanilla extract
½	teaspoon orange juice
1	teaspoon almond extract
3⅓	cups all-purpose flour
2	teaspoons baking powder
1	cup chopped almonds or nuts of your choice

Preheat the oven to 325°F.

In a large bowl, beat the eggs and sugar together at high speed with an electric mixer for 5 minutes, or until foamy. Add the orange zest, oil, vanilla, orange juice, and almond extract, beating until blended. Sift the flour and baking powder together and add to the sugar mixture, beating well. Fold in the almonds by hand. Cover the dough in the mixing bowl and place in the freezer for 30 minutes or in the refrigerator 2 hours until firm.

Divide the dough in half. Shape each portion into a 5 x 8-inch log on a lightly greased baking sheet. Bake for 25 minutes or until firm. Cool the dough logs on the baking sheet for 5 minutes, then transfer to wire racks to cool completely.

Using a serrated knife, cut each log diagonally into ½-inch slices. Return the biscotti to the greased baking sheets and bake for 15 minutes. Turn the cookies over and bake for 15 more minutes. Cool on wire racks.

Home-Churned
Ice Cream

Makes
3½ quarts

When we were children, we never made homemade ice cream unless we had company. I'm not sure if it was because we were being sociable or if it was because we needed help with the old hand churn. After working that hard, you definitely deserved a big bowl of ice cream! Daddy always added fresh peaches to this recipe because he loved homemade peach ice cream. Feel free to experiment with a fruit *you* love. I usually make it plain, then put out bowls of peaches, strawberries, bananas, nuts, and chocolate syrup so my guests can top it as they please.

- 2 recipes Boiled Custard, chilled (page 215)
- 1 pint fresh fruit, such as fresh Georgia peaches, peeled, pitted, and mashed
- 6 cups whole milk
- 20 pounds crushed ice
- 3 pounds rock salt

Wash the can, lid, and dasher of a tall 1-gallon electric or hand-cranked ice cream churn with hot soapy water. Rinse with cool water. In a bowl, mix the custard with the fruit. Set the dasher into the freezer can and pour in the fruit and custard. Add milk to within 3 inches of the top of the can or to the fill line marked on your freezer can. Put the lid on the can and place it in the freezer pail, making sure to center the can on the raised can rest in the bottom. Put several handfuls of ice around the can to hold it upright. Attach the motor or hand crank.

Start the motor of an electric churn and begin packing the space around the can with ice and salt, starting with about 4 inches ice and then adding about 4 ounces (½ cup) rock salt. Continue adding ice

continued . . .

and salt in this manner until the ice reaches the top but does not cover the top of the can. Add 1 cup cold water to help the ice begin to melt. The freezer pail should be placed in a large pan or sink so the salt water that drains out does not damage surfaces. Make sure the drainage hole stays open.

Freezing takes 20 to 30 minutes. Add more ice and salt as needed. An electric churn will stop when the ice cream is frozen. If the motor stalls too soon, unplug it and check to be sure no ice is caught between the bottom of the can and the freezer. Do this by using your hands to force the can to turn and then restart the churn. A hand churn takes about the same amount of time; you will know it is frozen when the churn becomes very difficult to turn.

Wipe away any ice and salt from the lid of the can and carefully

remove the lid. Pushing down on the can, carefully pull out the dasher, scraping any clinging ice cream back into the can. At this stage, the ice cream is soft. Put the provided cork stopper into the hole in the lid and replace the lid.

Harden the ice cream by adding more ice and salt to the freezer bucket, completely covering the can and securely corked lid. Cover the freezer with a heavy towel or newspaper layers and store the churn in a cool place until ready to serve. If you are not serving the ice cream within 1 hour, remove the towel and pack more ice and salt in the freezer pail. Dispose of the salt water in an area away from grass or plants. Scrub and rinse the pail thoroughly to avoid rust.

Boiled Custard

Boiled custard is a southern tradition that has been used for centuries in recipes like banana pudding, pies, and homemade ice cream. It adds the richness and flavor of a pastry cream to every recipe it's used in, but it's not as thick.

Makes 2½ cups

- 2 cups whole milk
- 6 tablespoons sugar
- 1 tablespoon cornstarch or 2 tablespoons all-purpose flour
  Pinch of salt
- 2 large eggs
- ½ teaspoon vanilla extract

From Gwen: Don't be turned off by the term *custard.* This is delicious served cold.

Heat 1½ cups of the milk in a double boiler until a skim forms (just before boiling) on the top of the milk.

Sift together the sugar, cornstarch, and salt in a mixing bowl. Stir in the remaining ½ cup milk.

Beat the eggs in a small bowl. Whisking constantly, slowly stream ¼ cup hot milk into the eggs.

Slowly pour the egg-milk mixture back into the double boiler, whisking constantly to prevent lumps. Stir in the sugar mixture and continue cooking the custard until it thickens, about 15 minutes, stirring constantly (see Note). Stir in the vanilla.

Note: Combining hot milk and eggs is a delicate process, and lumps may appear even if you are very careful. If lumps do appear, strain the custard through a fine sieve.

Blanche's Easy Ice Cream

Makes 1 gallon

From Gwen:
Beth and John requested this for their wedding rehearsal dinner in 1985.

I'm including this recipe from my sister's mother-in-law, Blanche (Whew! That's a mouthful!), because it is so easy, skips the time-consuming custard-making process of the previous recipe, and tastes awesome! Try both recipes and see which one you like best.

2   5 ½-ounce packages vanilla instant pudding/pie filling mix

3   cups sugar

8   cups whole milk

2   13-ounce cans evaporated milk

Combine the pudding mix and the sugar in a large bowl. Slowly stir in the milk. Continue stirring until the mixture is smooth. Pour the ice cream mixture into the 1-gallon canister of an electric ice cream freezer. Add milk if necessary to reach the fill line marked on the canister, leaving at least 3 inches of headspace. Follow the instructions for making Home-Churned Ice Cream (page 212).

Caramel Candy

This candy is a Christmas memory for me. Beth and I can hardly wait for it to cool every year so we can slice it up and wrap it. We always eat as much as we wrap (or more), so truthfully, I don't really know how much the recipe makes!

¾ cup (1½ sticks) butter

1 cup light brown sugar

1 cup granulated sugar

1 cup dark corn syrup

2 cups (1 pint) heavy cream

2 cups chopped pecans

1 teaspoon vanilla extract

Generously grease a 9 x 12 x 2-inch pan using ¼ cup (½ stick) of the butter.

In a large saucepan, mix the brown sugar, granulated sugar, corn syrup, and 1 cup of the cream. Heat until the mixture begins to boil. Slowly stream the remaining 1 cup cream into the mixture, stirring while it's boiling. Attach a candy thermometer to the pan and cook the mixture over medium heat until it reaches 244°F. Remove the pan from the heat and add the remaining ½ cup butter, the chopped pecans, and the vanilla. Pour the candy into the buttered pan.

Cool the candy in the refrigerator until it is just firm but not hard, about 1 hour. Cut into 1-inch squares. Cut waxed paper into 4-inch squares and wrap each piece of candy individually. Store in the refrigerator. Remove the candy from the refrigerator and allow it to soften slightly before serving. The wrapped candy's flavor is improved by aging in the refrigerator for 2 weeks.

Makes 6 to 7 dozen 1-inch cubes

From Gwen: The recipe in my file is written on the back of a mimeographed copy. Does anyone even remember the mimeograph machine? We retired teachers sure do.

Peanut Brittle

Georgia produces more peanuts than peaches—maybe it should be called the peanut state! This is one great way to use them. Daddy loved peanut brittle, and he made this all the time when I was growing up.

1 teaspoon vanilla extract

1 teaspoon baking soda

1 teaspoon salt

1 cup (2 sticks) butter

3 cups sugar

1 cup light corn syrup

3 cups shelled raw peanuts

Measure the vanilla into a small bowl and set aside. Combine the baking soda and salt in another small bowl and set aside. Butter 2 jelly roll pans or cookie sheets with sides liberally with the butter, using ½ stick butter on each one. Set aside.

Combine the sugar, corn syrup, and ½ cup water in a large saucepan. Bring the mixture to a boil, attach a candy thermometer, and cook over medium-high heat until the syrup spins a thread when poured from a spoon or reaches 240°F on the thermometer. Stir in the peanuts and continue cooking and stirring until the candy becomes golden brown or reaches 300°F. Remove from the heat immediately and quickly add the remaining 1 stick butter and the vanilla, baking soda, and salt. Stir only until the butter melts, then quickly pour the brittle onto the cookie sheets, spreading the mixture thinly. When the brittle has completely cooled, break the candy into pieces and store in a tightly covered container.

Colleen's Chocolate Fudge

Garth's mom was famous for her fudge, and I feel honored to include her recipe in this cookbook. I think that one of her secrets was the old, deep cast-iron skillet she used to make it in. I know the peanut butter makes it really smooth!

½ cup (1 stick) butter

3 cups sugar

⅔ cup cocoa

1 teaspoon salt

1½ cups milk

½ cup smooth peanut butter

1 cup chopped pecans

2 teaspoons vanilla extract

Makes 24 pieces

From Trisha: Use whole milk in this fudge to make it extra creamy.

Coat an 8 x 8-inch pan or platter with 4 tablespoons of butter. In a medium saucepan, stir together the sugar, cocoa, and salt. Stir in the milk. Bring the mixture to a rolling boil and reduce the heat to medium-low. Attach a candy thermometer to the saucepan and continue to simmer for 25 to 30 minutes, or until the mixture reaches 240°F or a drop of the mixture forms a soft ball when dropped into cold water. Remove the pan from the heat, stir in 4 tablespoons butter, the peanut butter, the pecans, and the vanilla. Pour the fudge out onto the buttered pan or platter. Let the fudge cool on the platter for 20 minutes, then cut it into bite-size pieces.

thanks

Wow! Putting together a cookbook entails so much more than just finding some recipes you like and sticking them in a notebook! To everyone at Clarkson Potter, especially Pam Krauss, for helping make this dream into a beautiful reality (and for teaching me all the cool publishing lingo!), and Jennifer Beal, thank you for designing this lovely book. Kate Tyler, Sydney Webber, Jane Treuhaft, Patricia Bozza, Joan Denman, Merri Ann Morrell, and Lauren Shakely: Your talents are greatly appreciated! Kathleen Fleury, thank you for always keeping me in the loop, and closing the gap between New York and Oklahoma! Special thanks to Ken Levitan and Vector Management for making it all happen.

I never knew a photograph of food could make me so hungry! Ben Fink, thank you for making our simple food look so divine. I knew I loved you the minute you said we could eat the food right after we photographed it! Special thanks to Jeff Kavanaugh, Philippa Brathwaite, and Susan Sugarman for photographing, styling, and preparing everything necessary for these photos. Thank you to Russ Harrington for shooting the cover. Melissa Perry, thank you for cooking every one of these recipes and reminding me every day that directions in my head needed to be written down on paper! Thanks to Debra Wingo, Mary Beth Felts, Claudia Fowler, and Sheri McCoy-Haynes for hair, makeup, wardrobe, and helping decorate tables and eat food!

Thank you to the people of Monticello, Georgia, who gave their time, location (thanks for letting us use your pond, Joanne Jordan!), a place to stay (thanks Mr. Chick and Mrs. Mary Ellen Wilson, and the Monticello Motel!), setting up picnic tables and getting the house ready (Kathryn and James Sauls, and George Deraney), and Sherry Partenza for the catfish!

Thank you to the friends and family who contributed recipes and stories for this cookbook: Margaret Akins, Jan Anderson, Blanche Bernard, the Bernard family, the Brooks family, Leslie Cromer, the Geissler family, Jarrah Herter, Herb and Glenda Hickey, Kathy Alexandra Hicks, Betty Hudson, the LeFlore family, Betty Maxwell, Wilson and Beth Paulk, Julianne Perry, Phyllis Pritchett, Jodi Roberts, Venita Sandifer, Gail Shoup, Donald and Patti Shuford, Mari Smith, the Smittle Family, Maria Smoot, Violet Steinke, and Jean Williamson.

Lastly, a big thank-you to my mom, Gwen, and my sister, Beth. What an adventure! We did it, and it's finally here! I love you both so much and am so proud that we got to do this together.

index